THE M
ENCOURAGING BOOK
ON HELL EVER

Thor Ramsey

"It must be understood, that there is risen up, now at length in this happy age of light and liberty, a set of men, of a more free and generous turn of mind, a more inquisitive genius, and a better discernment." [1]
– Jonathan Edwards, during a rare moment of sarcasm, referring to the church leaders of his age who were reinventing the doctrines of historic Christianity

"You're not going to believe this, Mr. Edwards, but it's happening again."
– Thor Ramsey, customarily sarcastic

CruciformPress

"Is the fear of God merely an Old-Testament doctrine? Does hell glorify God? Will we party with Pol Pot, Vlad the Impaler, Stalin, the Marquis de Sade, and Satan in heaven? And what about Bill Maher? For answers to these and other questions, this thought-provoking, bracing corrective to the soapy bromides of recent volumes on this subject may be just the ticket. And have we mentioned that it's entertaining *and* encouraging?"

– **Eric Metaxas**, New York Times Best-selling author of *Bonhoeffer: Pastor, Martyr, Prophet, Spy*

"*The Most Encouraging Book on Hell Ever* is also one of the wisest. This book is crammed with hilarious quips ("Where do Universalists tell people to go when they're angry?"), but the message is deadly serious. Losing the doctrine of hell isn't trivial. It means losing truth, righteousness, and grace. Ultimately it means losing God. Thor's book uses humor to disarm readers just enough to deliver this crucial and timely message."

– **Drew Dyck**, Managing Editor, *Leadership Journal*

"Praise God for Thor! The end must be getting near as Christians are actually getting funny. After a few pages, you'll realize this ain't your grandma's book about hell… but she'd love it just the same. Because it's only funny in the right places."

– **Stephen Baldwin**, actor, author, radio host

Dedication

Dedicating a book on hell is problematic. Which ex-girlfriend do you choose? To avoid any further threats of litigation, this book is dedicated to all the pastors who act like men, friends who stick, enemies who point, financial gurus with trademarked names, rock band members who read, rappers who preach, countrymen who think, illegal aliens who pray, widows who weep, guilty divorcees who repent, San Diego Chargers' coaches who win, doubtful Christians who seek, and lay people with discernment—especially those from Grand Rapids, Michigan who find grace disabled by sentimental views of a morally lax and complacent God who winks at evil and has about as much authoritative oomph as the public school system's bus drivers, not that they don't do the best they can to keep the little tyrants in order.

May you all begin speaking about eternal punishment again with tenderness and clarity.

Especially the bus drivers.

–Thor Ramsey

CruciformPress

Our Books: Short and to the point—about 100 pages. Clear. Concise. Helpful. Inspiring. Easy to read. Solid authors. Gospel-focused.

Multiple formats: Print and the three top ebook formats.

Consistent Pricing: Every title the same low price.

Website Discounts:

Print Books (list price $9.99)

1-5 Books	$8.45 each
6-50 Books	$7.45 each
More than 50 Books	$6.45 each

Ebooks (list price $7.50)

Single Ebooks	$5.45 each
Bundles of 7 Ebooks	$35.00
Ebook Distribution Program	6 pricing levels

Subscription Options: If you choose, print books or ebooks delivered to you on a schedule, at a discount.

Print Book Subscription *(list $9.99)*	$6.49 each
Ebook Subscription *(list $7.50)*	$3.99 each

---

The Most Encouraging Book on Hell EVER

Print / PDF **ISBN:** 978-1-936760-82-4   ePub **ISBN**: 978-1-936760-84-8
Mobipocket **ISBN:** 978-1-936760-83-1

Table of Contents

HOW TO READ THIS BOOK

First, pay for it.

Thank you.

Second, as philosopher Mortimer Adler has aptly explained, any source other than the original is inferior. So as you read this book, look up the Scriptures — go to the original source and interact with the Bible.

Third, while there's no poetry in this book, this doesn't mean couples can't read it aloud to each other on date night.

A few more thoughts…

Every Sunday, I address four different types of people. Now, if you don't like being categorized, brace yourself because I'm about to categorize you. Sitting in the pews (or stackable chairs) each Sunday morning are Christians who are sincerely pursuing Christ, Christians who have grown cold in their relationship with Christ, people who think they are Christians but are not, and people who know they are not Christians but are open to hearing about Jesus and the gospel.

If you happen to be in the last category, someone who knows they are not a Christian, there are two ways you can read the Bible. One, you can read it with a prove-it-to-me attitude. This is never a helpful way to read anything, especially sacred writ. None of us comes to God on our own terms. Without often realizing it, many of us want God to jump through our hoops. As long as God meets our requirements for an acting deity, then sure, we'll believe. But I can guarantee that you won't find God by using that kind of mindset. The silence will remain—simply, because God is opposed to the proud. The reality is that if you truly want to know God it is always on his terms. That is why you will find that in this book I have not made anything about the doctrine of hell more palatable to you. It's pulled straight from the Bible without whitewash.

The other way you can read is with a humble attitude that says, "God, if Jesus is the truth, if this is the way, show me, and I'll follow you." He will show you the truth of the gospel on his terms—simply, because God gives grace to the humble.

If you happen to be a tentative Christian, and the doctrine of hell stumbles you, then read with that same humble attitude, and I pray the Lord will bring you to a deeper conviction of the truth of his Word and your understanding of it.

If you're the Christian who is spiritually cold, then I suspect some caring friend gave you this book. Thank your friend for me, first of all, for buying the book. Second, be thankful you have a friend who cares. (Now, if you received this book, and you're not spiritually cold, rejoice, because you just got a free book!)

If you think you're a Christian, but you're not—well, find out now and then become a Christian. That's a great idea.

If you're a pastor, I've left you some encouraging words at the end of the book.

If you're a child, I'm guessing you're probably home-schooled.

INTRODUCTION
WHAT DO WE REALLY LOSE IF HELL FREEZES OVER?

Or Why Hell is a Good Idea

Hell, the doctrine of eternal punishment, misery without end, or as it's often referred to, "mother is moving in with us," is not very popular these days. On second thought, I can't think of a time when the doctrine of eternal punishment was popular (not that I don't personally enjoy my mother-in-law's visits). In today's age of peace, love, and misinformation, the subject of hell seems to make church leaders sweat even when they're not trying to be ironic.

In response, there is a swath of fashionable new preachers with a mission to clean up God's nasty reputation as a bloodthirsty old clod. Unfortunately, in the process of doing God the big favor of helping with his PR, they're reinventing the doctrine of eternal punishment with a new and improved gospel. It's gospel-riffic! Despite two thousand years of historic Christian interpretation, these new gospel hucksters are questioning whether Jesus spoke of hell as a real place of eternal suffering and torment at all. But if hell isn't real, and only a warning, the biblical authors could just as well have penned, "You better not pout, you better not cry." It becomes a hollow warning with about as much sway as a shopping-mall Santa.

"Be good, kids."

"You smell like beef and cheese."

Buddy the Elf's rebuke could be applied to these new teachers of hell as well: "You sit on a throne of lies."

Hell's Makeover Assistants

It seems as though Christians are always trying to help God out and explain hell (and other unseemly doctrines) in more culturally acceptable ways. People often listen to anyone who will tickle their ears with a new, softer theological feather. The one tricky thing that these preachers have in common is they say the name of Jesus a lot. Sure, they want you to follow Jesus and if you don't…well, that's it. Nothing, really. *Thanks for coming. See you next Christmas.* No hellfire and brimstone. Just love and lattes. The new doctrine of hell, as you'll see, is simply not effective: "Repent or…nothing of serious consequence will happen to you."

One opponent of eternal punishment said that if God punishes people with eternal retribution, then God is a monster. And if God is not a monster, then you are a monster for believing it. But look, if we all end up in heaven, it doesn't really matter if we're monsters or not, now does it? Actually Jesus taught the doctrine of eternal punishment because we *are* monsters. I have former girlfriends who will confirm as much.

Another bestselling Christian author says more of

the same in his book: the preaching or teaching of hell is "misguided and toxic and ultimately subverts the contagious spread of Jesus' message of love, peace, forgiveness, and joy that our world so desperately needs to hear."[2] If his viewpoint is true—that ultimately everyone ends up in heaven—then preaching eternal punishment subverts nothing. If we all end up in heaven, why do we even need to find forgiveness here on earth? Even us monsters who believe in hell will end up in heaven.

I find it interesting that many contemporary preachers want to save people from the idea of hell, rather than from hell itself.

The doctrine of hell is treated like the Christian's dirty little secret—the pock mark on the church's history formed during its teenage years. Maybe Christians are afraid that if we preach hell, people will think we're ignorant and simple-minded. (Thankfully, people today no longer think Christians are ignorant and simple-minded. They think we're ignorant and narrow-minded.) As we lose sleep over social ostracism, down at the neighborhood Target popular books on nuovo hell (or as the French would say, nouveau hell) line the racks claiming Christianity is compatible with postmodern sensibilities with an aim to make Christianity cooler. But the single most troubling idea regurgitated by many of today's authors is a second chance in hell after death. This amounts to Christian universalism.

The Strange Universe of Christian Universalism

Universalism is the belief that everyone will eventually be saved from hell (or just go straight to heaven, period).

Many fashionable evangelicals profess to believe in hell, but it's a sort of air-conditioned hell.[3] I would include in this idea of universalism John Stott's school of annihilationism (that God destroys the souls of the unrepentant), which effectively does away with hell altogether.[4] Who needs air-conditioning? Save electricity. At least annihilationism is green, which is the one positive thing I can say about it.

There are several variations of Christian universalism. One idea claims that everyone is already saved unless they choose not to be saved.[5] As in, you're already in unless you choose to opt out. You might be saved, but you just don't know it. If you remain ignorant, I guess there's no chance of opting out of hell. If this is the case then we should just shut up about this whole gospel business before someone accidentally loses his salvation.

Another thread of Christian universalism suggests that hell may not be the last word. There might be a word after that, and the word is that you eventually get into heaven.

Clearly, proponents of these ideas have not come to terms with the greatest drawback to universalism: where do Universalists tell people to go when they're really mad at them? "Why don't you just go to…ah, I guess I'll see you later."

It has been said, "Anyone who is not a Universalist should be at the very least a Universalist sympathizer."[6] But promoting the idea that hell might not be the last word after you die is only good news for people involved in the great insurrection against God. It's great news for parents who neglected their kids; for dads who deserted their families and moms who didn't protect their children;

for the pirates of the Caribbean and the pirates of Wall Street; for Hitler and Stalin and Vlad the Impaler. So much for justice sympathizers.

Before jumping to conclusions about whether hell is a reasonable doctrine or not, every professing Christian ought to consider what Scripture says about the nature and character of God. The author of Deuteronomy writes: "His work is perfect, for all his ways are justice" (Deuteronomy 32:4). The Psalmist writes, "This God — his way is perfect; the word of the LORD proves true" (Psalm 18:30).

The Jagged Little Pills of Scripture

According to the witness of Scripture, every Christian should affirm that God is perfect in all his ways and will glorify himself in all he does. If this is true (and I'm betting my life it is), surely there are doctrines that will be difficult to swallow. The issue with any difficult biblical doctrine (election, predestination, reprobation, eternal damnation, etc.) is that we are finite beings who don't know what the next thirty seconds will bring. Yet somehow we always think we know better than an infinite, holy, and all-wise God. The self-revealed God of this universe does not shuffle his feet or mince his words regarding hell. But the way the subject of hell has been handled of late, these teachers would have us believe God was second-guessing himself. As if he were saying, "Yeah, I wish there was another way. I know hell seems mean and all, but my hands are tied. Sorry about your nana."

We may waffle on the difficult doctrines, but God does not.

This might seem shocking to you, but I delight in the doctrine of hell. Let me explain myself before you tell me to go there. I didn't arrive at this mindset overnight, but now I delight in everything that God has revealed to us about himself. Any glimpse into the workings of the mind of God should delight a Christian. Now, this doesn't mean I've made a list of people who've wronged me and gleefully look it over thinking, "You'll get yours." The Bible clearly says, "Have I any pleasure in the death of the wicked, declares the Lord GOD, and not rather that he should turn from his way and live?" (Ezekiel 18:23). But just because it's a difficult doctrine doesn't mean the church should be embarrassed by it. I have slowly come to realize that to be embarrassed of hell is to be embarrassed of God.

When I began studying the doctrine of eternal punishment, I had this thought but I couldn't bring myself to say it out loud. It sounded absurd. It was too shocking to think, let alone say out loud. The thought was this:

Hell glorifies God.

I know. Exactly. It's the halitosis of theological thinking, but it is truth nonetheless. And that is the simple premise for this book: hell glorifies God.

That's why I take delight in it.

I know it's shocking. I know it raises some questions. Personally, one of the things I love about the Christian faith is that it's always shocking me with something. Reformed and always reforming. Yes and amen. But also, shocked and always shocking.

How could anyone ever be an endless-punishment sympathizer? How can eternal punishment glorify God? The answer is pretty simple, really. Because belief in hell affirms the holiness of God and other such attributes of his, like truth, righteousness, justice, and grace. Why do you think superheroes steal their slogans from us? Truth. There is one true God; he is righteous in all he does and in who he is. God will bring justice to those who do not approve of him (which is the essence of sin) and who will not confess they have committed cosmic treason. There is justice for those who have been harmed by the unrepentant. And thanks be to God, there is grace for all us moral failures who turn to him in reverence, fear, and repentance. Grace is not the elimination of hell, and any idea that comforts people in their unrepentant state can in no way be loving, truthful, or gracious, and should be rejected (and this includes annihilationism).

These nuovo ideas are weak and shallow, because instead of wrestling with the paradoxes and complexities of the doctrine, they simply undermine the authority of the Bible. They may pay lip service to Scripture's authority, but as they reinvent hell, they're bringing the Bible's credibility down to a much lower level, something on par with Wikipedia's reliability.

They simply lack depth.

The aim of this book is not character assassination. Instead, I'd rather take Francis Schaeffer's recommendation when it comes to dealing with false teachers. And that is to focus on the false ideas, not the person. Let's not be ridiculous though. If you're familiar with the controversies surrounding this subject, you know the personalities involved. It's not that I'll never mention a name, but let's keep in mind that fifty years from now the names won't mean anything to anyone. The person is not the point. The bad theology is.

At the end of the day, to lose the doctrine of eternal punishment as it is taught in the Bible will result in the shrinkage of God's attributes and in the end, a smaller God. We will suffer the loss of the fear of God, the loss of a holy God, the loss of a just God, the loss of an extravagantly loving God, and the loss of God's wisdom in the cross. We can't afford to lose the attributes of God. Otherwise we have a meaningless gospel. But the greatest loss whenever Scripture is minimized is the loss of knowing the self-revealed God of this universe. The truth is, hell glorifies God.

Thus, *The Most Encouraging Book on Hell Ever*.

One
WE LOSE THE FEAR OF GOD

Death is Actually not Your Biggest Problem

The first death I remember, even before a family pet was able to train me for loss, was that of my grandmother. I was only 5 years old when Grandma crossed the great divide—a phrase that makes it sound like she was killed by a math problem. (All our euphemisms divulge our fears.) Because of my age, my parents didn't take me to the funeral, but my mother showed me a photograph of my grandmother in her coffin. I examined it carefully. There was my deflated-looking grandma, the life sucked out of her (one of the side-effects of death) with her hands gently folded across her lap. Is this the only pose for the dearly departed? Just once I'd like to see their arms bent with both thumbs up.

Still, I couldn't stop looking at the photo. I remember being both fascinated and frightened.

I asked my mom, "What happens when you die?"

My mother told me that Grandma went to heaven, but she didn't say it with much conviction so I never found it comforting. I'm not even sure it was death that frightened me. I sensed there was something even more frightening than death.

And it wasn't hell. It was, in reality, a fear of God.

A few years later, when I was 8, I argued over the existence of hell with a little relative named Eve of my approximate age and height. I can't remember what prompted the argument, but we so strongly disagreed with each other that I said, "Let's go ask your mom." She warned me not to ask her mom. I pooh-poohed her warning and walked straight to her mother's doorstep and knocked. She was angry when she opened the door.

"This better be good," she said.

I thought it was good. Our eternal destinies seemed vital.

"We're having a fight," I told her. "I say there's a hell, and Eve says there isn't." (It's ironic that her name was Eve. "Did God really say…?")

Eve's mother waved her hands dismissively, "This is what you disturb me for? Hell? There's no hell!"

Then she shooed us away with some very strong words about her own wrath. We walked away from the doorstep without wisdom, though Eve had a face-splitting grin. Little Eve's grin said it all and was indicative of an entire cultural landscape: despite the biblical evidence, we'd rather make God in our own image.

Does God Need New PR?

Not all hell-talk among believers is as brazen as Eve and her mother would have it. Instead, some Christians just soft-pedal hell.

When I became a Christian during college, hell was gingerly called "separation from God," which sounded less scary than "eternal fire." Those that evangelized me tried to wrest the fear out of hell, but I knew what they meant. It was symbolically pictured right there in the diagram on the tract. I couldn't get across that bridge, but I knew what was underneath. I even understood the subtle euphemism, "separated from God," although at the time it never occurred to me to ask, "Where exactly can we escape God's presence?" Since no one ever spoke to me about hell in biblical terms, I had no idea that the thing that made hell hellish was the pouring out of God's wrath upon those being punished. I wonder now if those who evangelized me were being squeamish about giving it to me straight. Maybe they were hoping to do God a favor with his image by not overdoing the hell thing.

How do we round off the edges of eternal fire? Is there a room full of conference speakers out there somewhere brainstorming with a consulting PR firm?

"Wait a second! God makes hell hellish? I thought it was the devil. This will never do. Call in the marketing team. We need to change God's image. He's scary. Fear. Wrath. Hell. Any new ideas?"

"How about taking a *hell is helpful* angle?"

"I like where you're goin' with this! How is it helpful?"

"It cleanses."

"It's only temporary."

"Yes, yes, yes."

"Hell makes people see the error of their ways."

"And in the end…?"

"We all get saved!"

"Perfect!"

"We need to get this out right away. Call Target."

Fond Memories of Hell

There was a time when you couldn't sneak into an evangelical church without finding every head bowed and every eye closed. A piano would be playing a slow, soft tune in the background, accompanying the preacher while he gently instilled in the congregation a healthy fear of buses. "If you were hit by a bus walking home tonight (dramatic pause), do you know where you would spend eternity?"

It's still a valid question, but Christians don't ask it anymore because these days they feel the need to help God out with his bad reputation. Questions about where sinners will spend eternity sound unsophisticated and make people uncomfortable. Granted, the standard "If you were to die tonight, do you know where you would spend eternity?" isn't a great opener for funerals. That's what you close with, Goofy. Still, fear of God isn't what concerns our culture. It's death. And we can make a good case for this by simply culling an example from TV reruns.

The Last Laugh

There's an episode of *The Mary Tyler Moore Show* called "Chuckles Bites the Dust." In the episode, an employee of the TV station who plays Chuckles the Clown is on assignment one day at the circus. Dressed as a peanut, Chuckles the Clown is killed by an elephant. Though everyone loved Chuckles, they can't help making jokes about his death. They all find it troubling, but can't seem to stop making jokes. Lou Grant, Mary's boss, explains that it's "kind of a defense mechanism. It's like whistling in a graveyard. You try to make light of something because it scares you. We laugh at death because we know death will have the last laugh on us."[7]

Actually, Lou, death is not the thing to be feared—God is. The only thing that makes death fearful is facing almighty God. It all begins with the fear of the Lord. That's what I sensed as a child while looking at photos of my dead grandmother.

God should be feared in every sense of that word: from respect to esteem, from hallow to hold sacred, from adoration to awe, from trembling to terror, from dread to distress. When church leaders boldly say that they will either interpret away or ignore altogether any Bible verse that presents a God of wrath, it is painfully obvious that evangelicalism has lost the fear of the Lord.

The Fear of the Lord

Christians are not referred to as "God-fearing" any longer, even in self-referential ways, which is unfortunate because without the fear of God grace is unintelligible. Fear of God ought to be cultivated in pulpits and Sunday school curriculums. It teaches us wisdom, it makes us more humble, and it replaces all the folly in the human heart that is simply bent on sinful self-centeredness. Fear of the Lord is the lead-in for grace. Fascinating shellfish curses notwithstanding, the one major emphasis of the Old Testament is fear of the Lord. The emphasis of the New Testament is certainly grace. But also remember that the Old Testament makes up three-fourths of the Bible. This should tell us before we even get to grace that we should spend a very healthy amount of time expounding on the fear of the Lord. Fear of the Lord makes grace lucid. The apostle Paul expounds on the wrath of God in the book of Romans before he even mentions the grace of God in chapter five. We'd do well to do the same.

Fear of the Lord is Cultivated

Psalm 34:11 urges us, "Come, O children, listen to me; I will teach you the fear of the LORD," while in 2 Chronicles 26:5 Uzziah was "instructed…in the fear of God." If we stop cultivating a healthy fear of the Lord through shallow preaching and teaching, it will diminish among God's people. (Oh, it has. I guess we're here. Let's get to work.)

Fear of the Lord is Wise

The fear of the Lord is bound up with wisdom and knowledge. It is wisdom according to Job 28:28. It's the beginning of wisdom according to Psalm 111:10, Proverbs 1:7, and Proverbs 9:10. You can't argue with a trifecta of Bible verses! However, something to keep in mind, as author Jerry Bridges explains in his book *The Joy of Fearing God*, "Knowledge and wisdom are not the same, though they're closely related."[8] The best definition of wisdom I've ever heard is that wisdom is the ability to use the knowledge you have in a practical way. So, before you can have any wisdom, you have to have some knowledge. Wisdom is the right application of knowledge. This is why a person of inferior intelligence can be wiser than someone of superior intelligence. The simple person who applies the Word of God is often wiser than the smarter person who doesn't know or apply the Word of God. There is no greater stupidity than a stupid intellectual. Besides, fearing God safeguards us from becoming puffed up by our knowledge, because when the wisdom of God is in view we understand that we never know as much as we think we do. This leads us to…

Fear of the Lord Produces Humility

Humble people are teachable people. People who do not
fear God do not listen to him. "The fear of the LORD is
instruction in wisdom, and humility comes before honor"
(Proverbs 15:33). Humble people know that there are
truths in God's Word that may trump their own natural
inclinations. Humble people are "conscious of their
limited facilities, their ignorance of divine things, and their
proneness to err through depravity and prejudice" and
therefore they can be "induced to sit at the feet of Jesus
and learn of Him."[9] That is why they are teachable. They
are conscious of their limited knowledge regarding both
natural and spiritual things. The know-it-all is always a
fool, which leads us to…

The Folly of "Listening to Your Heart"

The flip side of the fear of the Lord and the humility it
produces is the notion of "following your heart." This
is something we're told to do by romance novels and
Lifetime movies, and it's the worst advice you can ever
be given. According to Jeremiah, "The heart is deceitful
above all things, and desperately sick; who can understand
it?" (Jeremiah 17:9). The deceitful heart is often the reason
women sometimes end up marrying mean drunks, but leave
my mother out of this. The point is, we need new hearts.
By all means, don't follow your heart. Theologian Michael
Horton has stated that the thing we all need to be saved from
is our subjectivity. And as I look deep into my soul…wait,
no! Look to the Word of God. God has given the Christian
a new heart which recognizes the truth of Scripture, which is
a light unto our path. Not our hearts, but the Word. Christians delight in the Word of God, which leads us to…

The Idolatry of "Doing Whatever Makes You Happy"

Right behind the "follow your heart" descent into subjectivity is the old adage, "do whatever makes you happy." The self-fulfillment ethic is the opposite of God's glory and the epitome of self-glory—one of the greatest idols of our age. The apostle Paul quotes Psalm 36 to describe the state of humanity, by saying that none seek righteousness or have the fear of God before their eyes (Romans 3:18). Christians understand (or should) that life is not bound up in whatever makes them happy; it's whatever makes God happy. The irony is that when you concern yourself with what delights God, you find yourself happiest. The Christian understands that he's made himself miserable by trying to make himself happy. He's made himself miserable by following his own wisdom. That's why he has changed his mind about "following his heart" and now follows God's wisdom in God's Word instead. And in doing so he has discovered happiness as the byproduct of obeying God. People who love God find their greatest joy in making him happy. If this idea doesn't make sense to you, well, I hate to break the bad news to you, but it's probably a good sign that you may not have a new heart—meaning, you may not be a Christian, my friend. My advice to you is to embrace a healthy fear of God, the real and living God, which leads us to…

Lack of Fear Creates Mythical Gods

Our culture (and much of the church) seems to prefer an alternative, sentimentalized, Santa Claus god who doesn't judge anyone. This imposter god is not good for humanity. This sham deity may seem much more compassionate than the God of the Bible, but instead, this type of god makes us less humane. Let me paint a vivid picture for you to illustrate my point.

The Inhumanity of an Unjust God

My father died when I was 11. During my freshmen year of college my mother got remarried, to a mean drunk. (What's ironic is that she was sober at the time.) Like most college kids, I came home for the summer months and there were times when my mother's mean-drunk husband and I clashed. Years later I found out that when I did something to upset him, instead of confronting me he would take my mom for a drive in the car and pound her thigh with his fist. This way no one would see the bruising. You have to plan ahead to be a coward.

In a universe where the sentimentalized, non judgmental, Santa-god reigns, all the mean drunks get away with it. Every single one of them. There is no justice for my mom or other abused women because there is no judgment, period.

But tell me this. If there is nothing more than a non judgmental Santa-god out there, why do human beings desire justice in the first place? If there is only a Santa-god, why do I both judge my mother's mean-drunk husband and condemn him in my heart? Woe is me…why can't I be more like Santa Claus?

The reality of this inner demand for justice means either a) It's sinful ever to judge under any circumstances, which amounts to being more like Santa, or b) I can experience righteous judgment in my heart because God created me in his image so I long for true justice, which amounts to being more like God.

If I see God as made in the image of Santa—meaning that there really isn't any justice in the world—then when I experience that God-given sense of justice I will be inclined to take justice into my own hands, and that's never a good thing. The mean drunk should be thankful that I don't believe in the no-justice Santa-god, because my emotional instinct is to take him out to coffee and shoot him, something even Starbucks frowns upon. Humans killing humans makes us less humane.

The Humanity of God's Wrath

Let's contrast this Santa-god with the biblical God of wrath who declares that vengeance is his, not mine. When my heart is captured by God's sense of love and justice, I realize that it's not ultimately my place to take my mother's mean-drunk ex-husband out to coffee and shoot him. I'm instructed to love my neighbor, turn the other cheek, and pray for my enemy, maybe even buy him a tall mocha-light, because my anger does not and will not produce the righteousness of God. So, I can withhold my own wrath, but only because I know my God won't let mean-drunk husbands get away with evil forever. (I'm not suggesting we should ever sit on the sidelines while someone is abused.) The mean-drunk husband will either be convicted by the grossness of his sin, repent, ask God for forgiveness, ask my mother for forgiveness, ask me for forgiveness, ask…trust me—there'll be a bunch of people in line for apologies. Or the wrath of God remains on him. In any case, he will ultimately receive justice, and as difficult as it is for me to withhold my own inferior (if more immediate) form of justice, I can trust God with the outcome.

Not only will God deal with the injustice of abusive spouses, but as I grow in the fear of the Lord myself, I realize that at one time the wrath of God abided on me, too. The only difference is that God's wrath toward me was absorbed by Jesus on the cross. Therefore, I don't giddily wait for God's judgment upon my mother's mean-drunk ex-husband. My hope is that he repents, believes the gospel, and receives mercy just like me. If it weren't for this realization, the aforementioned Starbucks shooting would be much more difficult to put out of my mind.

In a world where there are unrepentant mean drunks, the wrath of God is not only justified, but it makes him more worthy of our love and trust because, in the end, God doesn't let mean drunks get away with it. They either give their sin to Jesus, or in self-justification they hold onto their sin and incur God's wrath.

As Goes the Church, so Goes the Culture

When the church loses the fear of the Lord, so does the surrounding culture. But when we understand that God is to be feared, "we persuade others" (2 Corinthians 5:11). We understand the stakes when we're talking to someone who is, as the old-timers would put it, "careless for his soul." Evangelicalism's preference for Santa-god and a penchant for heart-following happy-thought-isms is opposed to where-will-you-spend-eternity-type truth-telling. People really have no idea how much danger they are in.

Contemporary preacher poets don't scare people with the wrath of God anymore. They lure people into becoming Christians with toothy promises of eternal life.

Fashionable preachers think the hellfire and brimstone preachers (the three that are left, anyway) are chasing people off. In reality, they're being faithfully prophetic.

Ezekiel writes, "Thus will I spend my wrath upon the wall and upon those who have smeared it with whitewash, And I will say to you, The wall is no more, nor those who smeared it, the prophets of Israel who prophesied concerning Jerusalem and saw visions of peace for her, when there was no peace" (Ezekiel 13:15-16).

Ezekiel's point is that there's actually something to worry about, and the non judgmental Santa-god is a whitewashed god. People will not throw themselves upon the mercy of Christ unless they see that they are completely deserving of the wrath to come. But that's not what we teach. Instead, we make Jesus out to be a buddy who plays softball in sandals or a career-catapulting life coach—not a crucified Savior and risen Lord. We trivialize what Jesus has done.

This trivialization of the cross is well put in a sermon titled "The Dark Garden,"[10] by Pastor Tim Keller. He says this:

> If there is no wrath by God on sin, and there is no such thing as hell, not only does that actually make what happened to Jesus inexplicable…it trivializes what he's done….If you get rid of a God who has wrath and hell, you've got a god who loves us in general, but that's not as loving as the God of the Bible, the God of Jesus Christ, who loves us with a costly love.
>
> Look what it cost. Look what he did. Look what he was taking. You get rid of wrath and hell, he's not

taking anything close to this. And therefore, what you've done is you've just turned his incredible act of love into just something very trivial, very small.

It's the difference between Jesus dying for you or just giving up his seat on the bus for you. May we repent of our trivializing of God's wrath, of our sentimental ideas of a false god, and rightly fear God for his love and justice as displayed in the cross.

Eve's mother's response, my mother's well-meaning but unconvincing answers regarding my grandmother's death when I was 5, death jokes about Chuckles the Clown, gun-shy evangelists, our culture's obsession with a non-judgmental Santa-god, the teachings of the nuovo Universalists, and Keller's astute observation of trivializing the cross all point to the same thing. When we lack fear of God, we end up fearing the wrong things.

Advantages of a Lingering Death

All these examples came full circle and culminated in a very truthful moment for me while listening to a lecturer from Duke Divinity School. Methodist theologian Stanley Hauerwas asked the audience how they would like to die. The responses ranged from "quickly" to "in my sleep" to "not on stage." (There was a comedian in the crowd.) Hauerwas then explained that medieval people feared a quick and sudden death because it would not give them time to be ministered to by the church. Armies even debated whether an ambush was immoral or not because it didn't give their opponents time to prepare for death. Medieval people wanted a lingering death because this would give them time to reconcile with their enemies. Does this mean they wanted to see their mother-in-law one last time? Of course not.

It means they didn't fear death.

Rather, they feared God.

Unlike many preachers today.

Who will not fear, O Lord, and glorify your name? For you alone are holy. All nations will come and worship you, for your righteous acts have been revealed.

(Revelation 15:4).

Two

WE LOSE THE
HOLINESS OF GOD

In All its Old-Fashioned, Bible-Thumping Scariness

My wife and I know of a little girl who was given
to a foster family when she was 2 years old. A homeless
woman found her alone in a park and called Child Protec-
tive Services. I'll call this little girl Sunshine (even though
her anonymity is probably the only thing that's been
protected in her short life so far). On numerous occasions
Sunshine's drug-addicted mother had left her in a park
for a full week at a time. Just think about that — a toddler,
alone, outdoors, for a week. Repeatedly. The mother told
CPS that her child was in the care of other women in the
park…other homeless drug addicts. These poor women
couldn't care for themselves, let alone someone else's child.

Having suffered the horrors of abandonment and
molestation, it's no surprise Sunshine was a problem child.
Her first temporary foster mother had such a difficult
time with her that she dropped her off at her second foster
home without even saying goodbye, only sarcastically
wishing the new foster mother, "Good luck."

Nothing provokes more outrage than sins against

innocent children. Well, unless the innocent child happens to have the unfortunate geographical location of the womb. The lack of outrage over such grotesque child killings as those uncovered by the Gosnell case reveals a culture that so smothers the truth that it yawns while children are slaughtered.

If you prefer a God without wrath, you prefer a God who winks at Dr. Gosnell.

You'd think that via super-nannies, higher-education ethics, and all the reality programming about wife swapping we would have learned compassion by now. Sadly though, children being treated like garbage is as old as sin. From the days when children were "dedicated" and burned to Molech at the Tophet in the Valley of Hinnom near Jerusalem,[11] to the present-day beheadings of babies in a doctor's office, to the opening of the nativity scene when Herod sent out the decree that every little boy 2 years and younger in Jerusalem and the surrounding vicinity be killed, the holocaust of innocent children is nothing new.

Merry Christmas.

Eliminate hell and we eliminate something vital to God's character, namely that our God is a consuming fire (Hebrews 12:29), completely holy, infinitely pure and righteous (Hebrews 1:9), a God who will not let the guilty go unpunished (Exodus 34:7). Eliminating hell changes who God is. Removing hell doesn't make God more loving. It makes him smaller, more like us. Thankfully, the gospel is about the good news that God is holy.

The God Like No Other

When we think of holiness we generally think of moral purity. And while holiness certainly has that connotation, there's more to it. To say God is holy is to say that God is separate, unique, like no other. The most iconic Bible verse of all time, John 3:16, refers to "God's one and only Son." "One and only" is another way of saying distinct, without peer. Jesus Christ, completely human, fully God, is like no other person who ever will be or ever was. And yes, he is flawless in moral purity, which goes hand in hand with being like no other. He is *holy*.

To be holy is, in a sense, to be a cut above. As R.C. Sproul put it, "He is an infinite cut above everything else."[12] So holiness is about both moral purity and transcendence.[13] Sproul explains: "Purity is not excluded from the idea of the holy; it is contained within it. But the point we must remember is that the idea of the holy is never exhausted by the idea of purity. It includes purity but is much more than that. It is purity and transcendence. It is a transcendent purity."[14]

God is matchless in holiness, and we are not. This poses some problems for us less-than-holy ones.

The God Who Hates Clichés

God hates sin because it is the exact opposite of his nature. The psalmist says, "For you are not a God who delights in wickedness; evil may not dwell with you" (Psalm 5:4).

It may surprise some to know that the Bible speaks more of God's anger, wrath, and fury than of his love, mercy, and grace. One reason for this (as we'll discuss in more detail later) is that love and hate are not mutually exclusive. It's because God is love (love is not God), that necessitates his hatred of evil—because sin and evil are an assault on his character and on his image-bearers.[15]

Unlike humanity, God never compromises with sin,

and hell expresses his final "no" to sin. A God who does not oppose sin is not holy. God hates war, exploitation, and oppression. He hates child pornography and neat suburban divorces. And he hates the claim that he approves of things he clearly condemns. God hates our sin because it's destructive to us and to others. He hates it because it offends his holiness. And he hates sin because it leads people to ignore the truth and misrepresent God (Romans 1).

What is the source of our sins? We are. This is why it's not really accurate to separate the sins from the sinner. Only the work of Christ at the cross can separate us from the due penalty of our own sin. Absent that, there is no separation between God's hatred of sin and his hatred of those who hold the guilt of their sin in their own hands.

Hating the Sinner in a Loving Way

Most of us have difficulty with the thought of God hating sinners because we see love and hate as absolutely incompatible. How can you love someone and hate them simultaneously? (Have you never been in a relationship?)

Throughout his ministry, pastor Richard Owen Roberts has often found himself in trouble for questioning the popular notion that God "hates the sin but loves the sinner." In a book every pastor in the known world should read, *Repentance: the First Word of the Gospel*, he writes,

> Sinners who love both their sins and themselves find it very pleasant to be told that God loves them just the way they are. It is delightful for them to be informed that it is only their sin that God despises. But statements of this sort only represent human traditions and are a long way from biblical truth.[16]

Everyone knows what it's like to experience a troubled conscience due to sin. But pastors who give false comfort to habitual sinners do them no favors. I agree with Roberts that God not only hates the sin, but he hates the sinner, too.

At this point you may be tempted to throw this book (handheld device?) across the room. Especially if that's where I'm sitting. But wait, please hear me out. Let's see what the Bible has to say first.

- "For you are not a God who delights in wickedness; evil may not dwell with you. The boastful shall not stand before your eyes; you hate all evildoers" (Psalm 5:4-5). *Evildoers* means sinners. It really is that simple. There is no reason to place evildoers and sinners into separate categories, unless you're designing an internet dating site. Biblically, sin and sinners are one and the same, but as we will see, we often compartmentalize and neatly separate them.
- "The LORD tests the righteous, but his soul hates the wicked and the one who loves violence" (Psalm 11:5). The wicked. Again, *sinners* qualifies as a synonym for *the wicked*. If God were separating the wicked from the wicked deed, he would have said so.
- "Everyone who is arrogant in heart is an abomination to the LORD; be assured, he will not go unpunished" (Proverbs 16:5). It doesn't say "arrogant deed." The arrogant *person* is the one being addressed. With old-fashioned Bible-thumping scariness, it's not just the sin of pride but the proud person who is an abomination to the Lord.

If you're tempted at this point to think God unjust, consider that the opposite is true—hell magnifies God's anger over *human* injustice. God's wrath highlights the reality of his love by showing us how much he hates not just sin, but also the perpetrators of sin, and that both belong in a special dumping-ground called hell.

As it turns out, love and hate are not mutually exclusive.

The God Who is Love also Hates

Theologian and philosopher John M. Frame is a master at stating deep thoughts in plain language. In *The Doctrine of God*, he explains, "The two (love and hate) are not always or in every respect incompatible. If love is a disposition to seek the good of someone else, and hate is opposition to the values and plans of someone, then it is certainly possible both to love and to hate the same person."[17]

That's what *ambivalence* means. Normally we use the word to mean the uncertainty of conflicting emotions. A more technical definition is the coexistence of positive and negative feelings. God, being like no other, can exhibit an unchanging love that is as strong as death—which is a pretty constant love because most dead people stay dead. And yet without the slightest hint of conflict, he can also exhibit a holy hatred toward those opposed to him. This means that God can simultaneously seek a sinner's best interests while opposing the sinner's primary motivations in life. God can both love the sinner by seeking his good while hating the wicked state of the sinner's heart.

We often think of love and hate as opposite ends of a linear spectrum. That's why many people see hate as only destructive, not as an appropriate and positive (hence loving) reaction. But the real linear spectrum at work here is one that has righteousness on one end and unrighteousness on the other. That's where the real separation lies. That is the true unbridgeable gap. Since God is righteous and loves righteousness it is only fitting that he exhibit a strong reaction against the moral opposite, unrighteousness. The God who is righteous hates unrighteousness.

In human terms, hate can be the aftermath of a great love betrayed. The person who loves you most is the person you have the most power to hurt. If God so loves us, then once we understand how completely we have betrayed him, we can better understand his hatred of us apart from Christ. (God's emotions don't have the shortcomings of human emotions, so while this isn't a perfect analogy, it's still a useful one.)

Who has loved us more than God? Genesis describes God's reaction to our betrayal by using the word *grieved* (Genesis 6:6), which in the original language carries the idea of being emotionally pained to the point of taking one's breath away. Now, the difference between humanity and God must be maintained here. That is, God is holy in that most underused definition of the word—again, "like no other." God is *other* than we are in every sense, including our emotional response. God's emotional response is not reactive, but always and only active, steady, and unrelenting. God has a constant, unchanging, active response toward sin that is completely compatible with his love.

Sin is evil because it's committed against God. There is no place for an arrogant humanity to snub even one request from a perfectly loving, infinitely holy, and all-wise God. That's why the apostle James wrote that if we are guilty of breaking one law we are guilty of breaking them all (James 2:10). Richard Owen Roberts answers one of the most common objections to God's zero-tolerance policy: "But perhaps you think, *That is not fair!*" Then another sin is immediately apparent in you. The sin of pride. Who do you think you are to declare to God Almighty what is fair and what is unfair? Nothing but pride would ever lead you to dare to speak against your Creator that way!"[18]

Therefore, God's hatred of everything and everyone in opposition to himself is clearly warranted because of who he is—the infinitely holy, righteous, perfect, good, wise, loving God of all things.

The problem is that we don't *really* believe we deserve God's wrath. This is akin to saying he's okay with our insurrection and our lack of devotion, which was the whole point of the story in the garden. Adam and Eve were given the pleasures of life, and yet gratitude *didn't* overwhelm them. Instead they sought to be the god of God, which is difficult to pull off because he is GOD! *That* is the story of humanity. We want to be the god of God, so much so that if we had the chance to put an end to God, we would.

Oh, that's right. We tried that already.

It's called the crucifixion.

God in Our Image

In our refusal to love God and instead embrace sin, we never quite see sin as an infinite evil. We usually think of our sins as minor hijinks. Hitler deserves hell but not us. It's always the other guy. Those "evildoers," they deserve hell. Not us "sinners."

In his book *Knowing God*, J.I. Packer accurately depicts American men and women (though you can freely apply this to the United Kingdom and Canada, especially those French Canadians):

> They tend to dismiss a bad conscience, in themselves as in others, as an unhealthy psychological freak, a sign of disease and mental aberration rather than an index of moral reality. For modern men and women are convinced that, despite all their little peccadilloes— drinking, gambling, reckless driving, sexual laxity, black and white lies, sharp practice in trading, dirty reading, and what have you—they are at heart thoroughly good folks. Then, as pagans do (and modern man's heart is pagan—make no mistake about that), they imagine God as a magnified image of themselves and assume that God shares his own complacency about himself. The thought of themselves as creatures fallen from God's image, rebels against God's rule, guilty and unclean in God's sight, fit only for God's condemnation, never enters their minds.[19]

Packer's point is that we think of God as "one of us." This is why the objection is often made, "My God would never send anyone to hell." To which we can only reply, "Obviously not, since your God is just a magnified image of yourself."

Sin in Our Image

God does not see sin the way we see it, precisely because he is holy—unlike any other. Most of us see sin as the breaking of rules, but this doesn't get to the heart of sin, which *is* the heart—the heart that sets itself above God's authority. God's rules do not exist in and of themselves. They derive from who he is. They point to him. God's rules are a reflection of his holy character. Thus, to snub the rules is to snub God. Ezekiel gets it absolutely right: "Because your heart is proud, and you have said, 'I am a god, I sit in the seat of the gods, in the heart of the seas,' yet you are but a man, and no god, though you make your heart like the heart of a god" (Ezekiel 28:2).

I once heard Tim Keller define sin as putting anything else in place of God. Therefore, all sin is idolatry. Idols are often even good things like family, spouse, leisure, or ministry work. Maybe drugs are your idol. Maybe it's prestige. Maybe *American Idol* is your idol. Or maybe you are your own idol. Whatever we choose as our object of worship indicates that we love something other than God. At the end of the day, we are our greatest idols, small gods who want to be THE God.

By the way, this self-idolizing thing makes us God's enemies.

They Hate the Church Because They Hate Jesus

Now you might be thinking, "I'm not God's enemy. I might not agree with your point of view, but I don't hate Jesus." If you don't currently happen to be a Christian, I can guarantee that when you're pressed about the gospel, your opposition to God will come burping out. Sometimes you don't even have to be pressed. I had dinner one night with Kevin, one of our church elders. He told me about his brother before he became a Christian. His brother exhibited strong opposition to Christianity with the slightest touch. One Saturday morning Kevin's brother called him and asked, "Whatta you up to today?"

Kevin answered, "Well, I've got a men's Bible study this morning, then I'm gonna head over to Home Depot…"

"Why do you always have to shove your religion down my throat?" his brother shouted.

Just mentioning a Bible study can seem like aggressive Christianity to some people.

The mere mention of God sets some people off because their sin is flagrant, and they cannot tolerate the notion of a holy God up in their business. Eternal punishment communicates in the most vivid way possible the utter holiness of almighty God.

Jeremiah 30:14 reads, "All your lovers have forgotten you; they care nothing for you; for I have dealt you the blow of an enemy, the punishment of a merciless foe, because your guilt is great, because your sins are flagrant." This is the condition of humanity. This was the sin of Herod when he slaughtered 2-year-old boys. This was the sin of the adults in Sunshine's life. This was the sin of Adam and Eve. This is our sin. Flagrant.

Insurrection against the King

Eternal condemnation takes sins against children more seriously than does an uncritical worldview that sentimentally proclaims everybody ends up in heaven as shiny, happy people. When we think of what was done to Sunshine — abandoned by her mother, molested by men in the park, and rejected by two foster homes — our hearts rise up with a cry for justice. When we think of a live baby struggling to swim in a toilet after an abortion procedure, we are outraged. If God did not display wrath against such wickedness, he would be unworthy of either our love or our respect. He would be a ruler unable to rule.

Imagine you are the subject of a King whose rule you have denied. In fact, you tried to have him killed and even declared yourself King. Now, being slightly less stupid than you are rebellious, you are hiding out in the forest in fear for your life. You know you have wronged this King. If caught you know you will be executed. And you know you deserve it. What you don't realize is that the King knows exactly where you are and could have you taken out at any moment.

Liken this for a moment to your state before you were a Christian (assuming you are one). Had you died as a non-Christian and been sent to hell, would you then have received what you deserved? Be careful, because it's a trick question. The answer is no. If you are the guy hiding in the forest from the King you deserve punishment from day one. Sinners deserve hell starting right now, not starting when they die.

Okay, back to you hiding in the forest…

One day when you're out hunting you come across a messenger of the King. He tells you, "I have amazing good news. The King has made a way to forgive you completely without harming the justice of his great name." Since this is a story about a human King capable of lying, let's just stipulate that he really means this. It's not a trick. Now that's pretty astonishing. The King acknowledges your wicked rebellion but is extending mercy and complete forgiveness in a way that maintains his justice.

That's a beautiful, powerful story that says a great deal about that King. Who the King is has been displayed in what he did on behalf of you, a rebel.

But what if the messenger said something else? What if he said, "Oh, I remember you. That insurrection thing? Yeah, don't worry about it. It's not a big deal. You should come back. You don't have to hide out here in the forest by yourself."

"What about the death sentence hanging over my head?"

"Aw, he didn't *really* mean it. He does this stuff all the time. You shouldn't take it too seriously."

That's not a King anyone can truly respect. That's not a King at all.

But Christ the King is more like the first King. Every moment you are hiding from this great King, you deserve death. The King knows where you are and can have you destroyed at any moment, but the great King is patient, not wanting you to perish. And all along you think hiding is working because you're not dead yet.

God Always Wins

Our exalted view of self has given us the idea that somehow we can win in our rebellion against God. But who are we, tiny humans, to refuse this God anything?

We cannot win. Yet we keep on fighting.

Just like Herod, we fear that the balance of power in our lives will be overturned, that God will usurp our (imaginary) authority and remove us from the throne of our heart. So in our arrogance we react like Herod: when God walked among us, and our self-deified kingdom became threatened, we decided to kill him. This is why the crowds yelled, "Crucify him! Crucify him!" We're in the crowd too… I'm reminded of the modern hymn that says, "Ashamed, I hear my mocking voice, call out among the scoffers."[20]

We crucified the King of glory because he threatened our kingdom of self. Then he rose again. And still, we moronically keep trying to do him in. As if we can somehow win against God.

If the modern, re-imagined view of hell is true, then sin is much less serious than the Bible makes it out to be. If it's true that eventually everyone ends up in heaven, then the child-molesting drug dealer will only have to spend a little bit of time in the fires of hell, but he'll be seeing you in heaven soon (assuming you've repented and believed the gospel).

Abandoning a toddler in the park is one thing. But it's enough. As Matthew 25:31–46 says:

> When the Son of Man comes in his glory, and all
> the angels with him, then he will sit on his glorious
> throne. Before him will be gathered all the nations,
> and he will separate people one from another as a
> shepherd separates the sheep from the goats. And
> he will place the sheep on his right, but the goats on
> the left. Then the King will say to those on his right,
> "Come, you who are blessed by my Father, inherit the
> kingdom prepared for you from the foundation of
> the world. For I was hungry and you gave me food, I
> was thirsty and you gave me drink, I was a stranger
> and you welcomed me, I was naked and you clothed
> me, I was sick and you visited me, I was in prison and
> you came to me." Then the righteous will answer
> him, saying, "Lord, when did we see you hungry and
> feed you, or thirsty and give you drink? And when
> did we see you a stranger and welcome you, or naked
> and clothe you? And when did we see you sick or

in prison and visit you?" And the King will answer
them, "Truly, I say to you, as you did it to one of the
least of these my brothers, you did it to me."

Then he will say to those on his left, "Depart
from me, you cursed, into the eternal fire prepared
for the devil and his angels. For I was hungry and you
gave me no food, I was thirsty and you gave me no
drink, I was a stranger and you did not welcome me,
naked and you did not clothe me, sick and in prison
and you did not visit me." Then they also will answer,
saying, "Lord, when did we see you hungry or thirsty
or a stranger or naked or sick or in prison, and did not
minister to you?" Then he will answer them, saying,
"Truly, I say to you, as you did not do it to one of the
least of these, you did not do it to me." And these will
go away into eternal punishment, but the righteous
into eternal life.

Whenever I read Jesus' parable of the sheep and
the goats I wilt inside. Whether the parable is about
humanity in general or more narrowly about fellow
Christians in need, it's a devastating indictment against
suspect Christian declarations. Either way, the proximity
principle is the same—to see great need in front of us and
ignore it is a great sin.

Never defend yourself against Scripture. God always
wins. Agree, weep, mourn, and repent.

Scripture is clear, but we don't like how it makes
us feel. So what do we do? We topple the authority of
Scripture and confuse its clarity, substituting speculation
for sound thinking. We reinterpret Jesus' words about
eternal punishment in a way that minimizes the serious-

ness of our own rebellion against God, including the kind of rebellion that results in abortion and child abuse.

Eternal punishment shows us that God takes sin—including sin against innocent children—seriously. Infinitely seriously. He does this because he is holy. Perfectly and infinitely holy.

It's a very encouraging thing to know that God is holy.

Three
WE LOSE THE
GOSPEL OF GOD

The Gospel Is Not about Escaping Hell, Though
This Is Highly Recommended

My dad died when I was eleven. I wanted to be a pallbearer, but this task was not to be trusted to a boy, even a husky one. Instead, all my dad's overweight farming buddies (with the exception of Earl Rungee, who weighed about eighty pounds with his pockets full of grain) lugged around his casket while huffing and puffing. I nearly expected the *Sioux City Journal*'s headline the next day to read: "Pallbearer Dies of Heart Attack While Carrying Casket of Man Who Died of Heart Attack."

Before my dad was taken to the gravesite, I looked at him in the open casket for a good long time. No one else was in the small church's sanctuary. They were all in the fellowship hall having a potluck, the pallbearers ingesting protein to boost their energy for the task ahead. I stood there alone and stared at my dad, knowing that everything was about to change with the loss of our most vital family member. (Who would do all the barbecuing now?)

Not long after, my mother sold our home and we

moved away. We only moved to the next city, but my
dad had been the vital connection to his side of the family.
When that connection was gone, they became distant.

The vital connection that had been my dad was lost,
so everything else changed. So it is with the gospel.

When hell is removed from the gospel, the gospel
becomes meaningless. This type of irreplaceable connection point is why the apostle Paul expressed himself so
passionately to the churches in the region of Galatia. He
wrote, "But even if we or an angel from heaven should
preach a gospel other than the one we preached to you, let
him be eternally condemned!" (Galatians 1:8, NIV).

To make sure they understood this wasn't just an
emotional outburst, he stressed it a second time: "As
we have already said, so now I say again: If anybody is
preaching to you a gospel other than what you accepted,
let him be eternally condemned!" (Galatians 1:9, NIV[21]).

From the context of Paul's words here, it appears
that eternal condemnation is part of the gospel. (Like in
the part where he writes, "eternally condemned.") Paul
was concerned about people's souls. He knew that losing
the integrity of the gospel equals a false gospel that leads
people to eternal condemnation.[22]

Read the New Testament carefully (you know, don't
skip parts) and you'll notice that Paul is in good company
when it comes to the topic of eternal condemnation.
Turns out the rest of the New Testament writers are in
agreement that hell is integral to the message of the gospel.
Maybe that's why every one of them writes about it. This
brings us to Paul's original condemnation in Galatians
and poses for us a fearful question. When popular church
leaders remove the teeth of eternal punishment, are they

not open to the same charges that Paul issued to the false teachers who were confusing the Galatians? Could some hipster pastors today be on the receiving end of a Jesus woe? "Woe to you lawyers! For you have taken away the key of knowledge. You did not enter yourselves, and you hindered those who were entering" (Luke 11:52).

Hell and the Purgatorial Bus Pass

Lots of people obviously die without any concern for God whatsoever, so in order to imagine a scenario where everyone goes to heaven, you have to push their salvation out beyond this life. Thus many of the new revisers of hell contend that it is only remedial. In effect, you take a really nasty purgatorial bus ride, like Greyhound with a better destination. I'm sure it's bumpy, and crowded with people who should never take off their shoes but do, and Keanu Reeves is driving and screaming about not being able to go slower than 50 mph or the bus will explode. But this particular hypothetical hell does have "good news"— once you see the error of your ways, there is an exit. My guess is that you pull the cord as an act of repentance, the bell rings, and as you hop off at the next stop Keanu says he was just kidding about the bus blowing up and hands you a transfer pass allowing you to jump on an express bus to the good and happy place.

In this scenario, the only real difference between Joseph Stalin and a hardened litterbug is how long they sit on the bus before they see the light. Everybody eventually changes buses.

If there are an infinite number of chances after death, then hell itself becomes the means of salvation rather than

Christ. So what did Christ die to save us from? A less happy life? Who can take seriously the Bible's warnings about rebelling against God if we all end up in heaven anyway?

Those who press this idea of a remedial hell claim that the death, burial, and resurrection of Christ is still efficacious in saving people from God's wrath. At the end of the bus ride (and, to be fair, the proponents of this view never actually use the word *bus*), people are still saved by what Christ did on the cross. But look, if the punishment in this version of hell is only temporary, then having a second chance in hell becomes a secondary "gospel." It's really a kind of backup gospel in case the first one proves inadequate. This both trashes the reliability of Scripture and encourages sin.

You know what else? It renders the Great Commission, to evangelize and make disciples in all the world, an essentially pointless exercise. As if just before he ascended back to the Father, Jesus gave his followers a bunch of busy work.

The same basic arguments against a remedial hell apply to the idea of annihilationism.[23] Rebellion against God is recast into something far less serious because one day you'll cease to exist anyway. What's to be scared of if you don't exist?

Annihilationism, remedial hell, it-only-seems-like-eternal torment (whatever you want to call your favorite nuovo hell, besides a colonoscopy)—if these views are true, all the biblical warnings and threats become nonsensical. If hell is merely temporary or all we face at death is a lights-out end-of-existence, it would be more logical for the biblical writers to be giving encouragements. "Sure it's hot. But only for a bit. It's really more like summer in Michigan, without the mosquitoes. Think of it as a really impactful *What I Learned on my Summer Vacation.*" If hell is temporary, the gospel doesn't actually get you out of anything besides a literal vacation in hell. So much for the good news.

I'm holding out for the greatest rescue mission story ever told, thank you. Because there *is* something truly at stake.

When Stories Matter

One of my best friends (even though he's Canadian) is named Leland. We have known each other for years. We're so tight, we even tell each other that we love each other (making sure we always add "man" at the end of the sentence). Imagine Leland and I are walking down the street and I say, "I want you to know how much your friendship means to me…man." Then I run out into traffic, get hit by a pickup truck, and die. Would Leland find such a display touching or would he check my pockets for drugs?[24] Now, imagine a different scenario where, after I express my moving sentiment, a car comes out of nowhere, jumps the curb, and heads straight for Leland. I push him out of the way and in the process plant my face in the car's grille. Now that's love put into heroic action. That's the kind of stuff that gives stories meaning.

Any high-concept, big-budget movie involves a hero saving the world. You know how it works. The movie can't just revolve around the need to save everybody living between 3rd and Maple in Dakota City, Nebraska (as wonderful as each of those particular individuals are, I'm sure). For a story to matter, the stakes must be high. The hero must at least have to save New York City, or America, or, you know, the planet.

The gospel is no different, except in this scenario *your* soul is at stake. If the death, burial, and resurrection of Jesus is not what saves us from the penalty and power of sin and ultimately from hell, as a result of Jesus standing as a substitute for sinners, then the purpose and meaning of the cross is more than a little fuzzy. It would be like me senselessly rushing out into oncoming traffic, as if that pointless sacrifice proved my love or really changed anything for the better.

The biblical facts remain. Human beings have truly sinned and truly incurred the wrath of God, but he has provided a way in the cross of Christ. That's why it's called the gospel—the good news that we're saved from our sin, hell, and the wrath of God.

The Non-Gospel

The nuovo teachers are repulsed by the idea of people being saved from God's wrath against sin. That is, they'd like the cross to be about something more pleasant, like Jesus the Great Inspirer of All Good and Enlightened People. They want us to rejoice in a cross that celebrates our good-enough-ness, a cross that shows us how the human spirit overcomes. Depravity-schmavity, they suggest. Instead of rejoicing that God objectively demonstrated love to us despite our sin, we're supposed to see the cross as God's disappointment with our poor choices and an encouragement to try harder to be more compassionate to relieve others of "hell on earth." Jesus certainly calls believers to lives of self-sacrificial love, but this nuovo-hell gospel—and any resulting good works it might produce—is not the true gospel. What it actually preaches is a moralistic salvation by inspiration of Jesus, our Good Example.

According to Paul in 1 Corinthians 15:

> Now I would remind you, brothers, of the gospel
> I preached to you, which you received, in which
> you stand, and by which you are being saved, if you
> hold fast to the word I preached to you—unless you
> believed in vain. For I delivered to you as of first
> importance what I also received: that Christ died for
> our sins in accordance with the Scriptures, that he was
> buried, that he was raised on the third day in accor-
> dance with the Scriptures (1 Corinthians 15:1-4).

Notice that the gospel is articulated as Christ dying
for our *sins*, not as an example that encourages us to more
sacrificial living. Sure, Christus Exemplar[25] is a legitimate doctrine, it's just not the content of the gospel. It's
true that the example of Jesus should inspire us to better
citizenship, but as Paul said with perfect clarity, what is of
first importance is Jesus' death and resurrection.

Meritorious works never save an individual or create
faith. Rather, in the new birth the Holy Spirit changes
hearts, which in turn effects change in a person's character,
which leads to new behavior and a God-glorifying life.
True, to not live a God-glorifying life—one characterized
by compassion, mercy, standing for justice and living with
integrity—is to make society worse.

But godly living and the good works of the individual
believer are not the gospel. They are the byproduct of
faith in the gospel. The content of the true gospel is not
about you, me, or the good works we do (or don't do).
Our works are all the good things that result because of
the good news, but they are not the good news itself.

Universalist sympathizers bring us a gospel of public opinion which turns out to be an impotent, me-focused, self-celebrating gospel that wants to highlight human good works and compassion. This old heresy made new presents a Christ who didn't pay for sins once and for all, but instead gives us a savior with a message to save yourself via inspiration rather than regeneration.

This is no savior at all.

Jesus Saves Us from Our Sins

To say that Jesus came to save his people from hell is fine as far as it goes, but if you leave it at that you've sold the gospel short. Jesus came to save his people "from their sins" (Matthew 1:21). Sure, that does save them from hell, but there's much more to it. The heart that's wrapped around greed, envy, lust, bitterness, lying, anger, hatred, selfishness, and all the rest is a heart that would be miserable in heaven. The declaration of the gospel is that Jesus saves us, not only from the penalty of our sins, but also from the dominating power of greed, envy, lust, bitterness, anger, and abusing and abandoning children—the very kind of hearts that produce what some call hell on earth. Hell on earth, indeed. But if not repented of, sin leads to an even worse hell—a hell of eternal conscious punishment in death. If you don't get saved from anything in this life, then you don't get saved from anything in the next life. But the point of it all isn't to avoid hell, it's to love God.

Jesus Diverts the Wrath of God

All this bristling at the thought of God's wrath is always an indicator of a low view of sin. And a low view of sin is always an indicator of a low view of God, because it doesn't take sin against him seriously. All sin is serious because it's committed against almighty God. All have loved sin and self rather than God and so deserve his wrath — the difference being that the unsaved will incur the wrath of God whereas God's wrath is diverted from the saved by Jesus. That's why they're saved.

> Since, therefore, we have now been justified by his blood, much more shall we be saved by him from the wrath of God (Romans 5:9).

> For they themselves report concerning us the kind of reception we had among you, and how you turned to God from idols to serve the living and true God, and to wait for his Son from heaven, whom he raised from the dead, Jesus who delivers us from the wrath to come (1 Thessalonians 1:9–10).

The Bible word for this diversion of wrath is *propitiation*. The American Heritage Dictionary defines this as "the appeasement and conciliation of an offended power, especially a sacrificial offering to a god." *Propitiate* is the only English word that gets across the idea of satisfying wrath by dealing with the penalty for the offense that caused the wrath. The difference between the pagan idea of propitiation and the Christian definition of propitiation is that in paganism *you* are the one who has to appease the gods with your offering, or your chanting, or your positive thinking, or your good karma, whereas in Christianity it is God who does everything, provides everything, secures everything.

Anyone who has ever been motivated by guilt is

someone who has tried to propitiate wrath. It's a useless endeavor in the pagan sense, because how many chants does it take to be justified (a legal term that means *to be declared not guilty*)? How much good do you have to do until you are actually justified—no longer guilty and therefore good enough for heaven? But the most important question is, how can you remove infinite guilt with temporal moral acts? None of this deals with the greatness of the offense. And this puts us squarely into the issue of eternal punishment again, because to die without having the propitiating, finished work of Christ applied to you means that *your guilt remains*. If you die guilty (unjustified), when will you be less guilty before God after you die?

That's right…never. Thus, eternal punishment.

The sin of our first parents in the garden amounted to spiritual suicide. Inheriting their guilt, we have also surely died. Now, if you commit suicide, you can't take it back. (Just a heads up.) You don't put the gun barrel in your mouth, pull the trigger, and then say, "On second thought." It's the same thing with rebelling against God. Once we've sinned against God, the deed is done. Our guilt remains. We don't get to take it back. As the apostle John writes in his gospel, "Whoever believes in the Son has eternal life; whoever does not obey the Son shall not see life, but the wrath of God remains on him" (John 3:36). Clearly, if sinners are to be reconciled to God, our guilt will have to be removed. We will have to be justified. The problem is that most people want to justify themselves. "I'm a good person, comparatively speaking, in light of Charles Manson and Adolf Hitler. Um…and as long as you can't see what's actually in my heart. Barring all that, I'm pretty good."

The Bible stresses that we cannot be saved by works

of righteousness. You can present your body to be burned as a martyr, you can sell all your possessions and give the money to the poor, you can drive a hybrid car with carpeting made from banana fibers, but none of these things will remove your guilt. Your guilt remains. You cannot propitiate the wrath of God by anything you do.

God Justifies Sinners in Christ

The uniqueness of Christianity is that our salvation isn't based upon anything we do, but upon everything God did in Christ. The gospel tells us that the Father initiated a plan with the Son whereby he poured out his wrath for our sins upon Christ instead of upon us. In love, the holy God thereby received justice *and* became the justifier, for all those who believe (Romans 3:26).

One of the clearest passages on justification was written by the apostle Paul, in his letter to the Galatians: "Yet we know that a person is not justified by works of the law but through faith in Jesus Christ, so we also have believed in Christ Jesus, in order to be justified by faith in Christ and not by works of the law, because by works of the law no one will be justified" (Galatians 2:16).

If that's a little unclear, let me try to summarize it by just pointing to that one part at the beginning, "A person is not justified by works of the law but through faith in Jesus Christ." Is that clearer? In this verse, Paul says the same thing three times. He's not suffering short-term memory issues; he's highlighting the extreme importance of his point—that Christ died *for* our sins, *in* our place, *removing* our guilt before God. In the gospel of Jesus Christ there is no room for vain regrets over past sins. All is removed. Clean. Cleansed. Crucified. God did it all.

Is it fair for God to punish some people eternally? That's the wrong question. *Is it fair for God to reward some rebels with eternal life?* Because that's exactly what he does in the gospel of Christ. He rewards those who deserve the exact opposite of what he gives them.

In the faddish model of the gospel minus hell, Christianity soon becomes a religion of "what's the point?" Now, I understand people will harp about love and justice and mercy as being the point, but these good works are *not the point.* The glory of God is the point. Social-justice issues along with all good works are just the outgrowth of a life that seeks to glorify God. Besides, in the version of the gospel minus hell the child abuser who never repents will also end up in heaven. I'm sorry, what was the point of all that justice and mercy and goodness again? Oh, you had a better life? Not according to the internet porn king who lives three doors down from you in heaven. Plus, this whole "you will have a better life as a Christian" argument is nothing but more selfishness in religious garb. Everyone wants their best life now, even Nazis. *Their* best life now was all about ethnic cleansing.

If Christianity is primarily about being good little boys and girls, what are we supposed to do with all that language in the Bible about sacrifice, propitiation, and justification in Christ? In the trendy model of the gospel, you don't need the cross to be made right with God. After all, in the purgatorial fires of hell, God will purify you, melt your heart, and bring you to the new earth. The stylish gospel sporting a temporary hell diminishes the cross of Jesus Christ and the glory of his work.

So the premise of this book stands. Take away the vital connection of Jesus saving his people from their sins, diverting the wrath of God, and pronouncing sinners justified, and you have a nonsensical gospel. Eternal punishment highlights the good news of the death, burial, and resurrection of Jesus Christ, and makes it more meaningful.

Thus, hell glorifies God.

Four
WE LOSE THE LOVE OF GOD

A Love Way Better than an Infinite Hug

Social critic and comedian Bill Hicks once said, "Christianity is such an odd religion. The whole image is eternal suffering awaits anyone who questions God's infinite love. *Believe or die.* Thank you for giving, Lord... for all those options."[26]

Years later, after Bill died tragically of pancreatic cancer (really the only way one dies of pancreatic cancer), the pastor of a large American church said nearly the same thing on the first edition of the back cover of his book: "God loves us. God offers us everlasting life by grace, freely, through no merit on our part. Unless you do not respond the right way. Then God will torture you forever. In hell. Huh?"[27]

Bill Hicks was a comedian. Comedians work in caricatures in order to write jokes, to get to the laugh before they die of pancreatic cancer. But why would a pastor use a misleading caricature? Pastors proclaim truth. That's the rumor, anyway. Unfortunately, evangelicalism is drawing too much from pop culture cues and has mostly communicated God's love in caricatures.

"God loves you just the way you are!"

"God's love for you is unconditional!"

These sentimental platitudes are so ingrained in our thinking that they're ultimately responsible for generating some of the most common questions asked about God's love such as, "How could hell be seen as flowing from the love of God?" Easy. Because God loves holiness and justice and righteousness and truth and goodness and etc. (We can assume that God loves the abbreviation *etc.* because he is infinite.) Hell makes a distinction between righteousness and unrighteousness, between justice and oppression, between gracious help and exploitation, between what God loves and what God hates, between submitting to his reign and rebelling against it.

The love of God detached from the gospel communicates nothing. If God loves everyone just the way they are, what's the point of repenting (turning around and going the other way) and believing the gospel? The reality is that God's love is much more complex than even a Woody Allen drama from his Ingmar Bergman period.

So, while believers and unbelievers can both struggle with harmonizing the love of God and the wrath of God, as we will see, sometimes hating is the loving thing to do. (But this doesn't mean your attitude about your mother-in-law is a good thing.)

The Sentimental Evangellyfish Gospel

The evangelical community has a long history of sentimentalizing the love of God, effectively divorcing it from his wrath (which of course effectively divorces it from everything else about him, including his holiness and justice). You could argue that this all started with the most popular man in America at one time, the Congregationalist preacher of the late 1800s, Henry Ward Beecher. The one-time orthodox preacher ended his ministry as a Universalist (again, the belief that everybody goes to heaven), which is what we generally end up believing when we can't get past shallow caricatures of God's love.

Beecher was one of the first American preachers to sermonize on the love of God almost exclusively, and because he knew how to capitalize on that he became a sensation. At the time, the nation was regularly browbeaten by hellfire-and-damnation preachers who drove people to despair that God would ever love them. Where Beecher preached love without wrath, these folks preached something just as damaging and biblically inaccurate: wrath without love. Not surprisingly, Beecher's much happier falsehood has dominated ever since. So much so that when someone offers a corrective, the backlash can get nasty, even when that corrective is the clear teaching of Scripture.

Go ahead. Try to offer some balance to that sentimentalized Christian bookstore coffee mug slogan, "God loves you just the way you are." You will typically be met with deep resistance. Well, let's hope those mugs don't cost too much, because I'm about to break them.

If God loves you just the way you are, there was no reason for Jesus to die on a cross for you. The point frequently missing from the gospel these days is that *God doesn't love you just the way you are*. Even if you are a Christian. And I mean a really, really great one. Instead, he loves Christ, and when you are found *in Christ*, then and only then do you find yourself in the absolute security of God's love. That's the glad tiding of great joy.

But this can never happen apart from Christ. Apart from Christ, God's wrath abides on you (see John 3:36).

Put that on a coffee mug.

God's wrath. "I don't believe in a God of wrath," someone says aloud while reading this book. I predict. But believe it or not, all of us not only believe in wrath, we admire it and even insist on it. All of us. Often we admire it when it shows up in the form of what we currently call social justice. The decision to alleviate an injustice in the world comes from being fed up, and by God (literally) we're going to do something about it. That's a certain kind of righteous anger, otherwise known as wrath. No, it's not exactly like God's perfect wrath, but it is a variation on the real thing.

When we hear of an individual, for example, who has dedicated her life to fighting sex-trafficking, we commend her pursuit of social justice. And when a lawyer labors in an organization committed to bringing the perpetrators of this trade to justice, we say amen (something people almost never say when lawyers are involved). Both of these individuals have a "wrath" against sex-trafficking, and we admire them for it.

That's a positive take on human wrath. Hating really can be the loving thing to do.

By contrast, most of our images of wrath tend toward Disney-esque depictions. You know, Sleeping Beauty's evil stepmother-type wrath. But God's wrath is not an emotional outburst over unreasonable jealousies provoked by a tell-all mirror. It is not petty rage or pee-vishness over some minor inconvenience—such as when you pull out into traffic and cause another driver to slow down, so you experience the wrath of the horn.

God's wrath is the execution of his justice — *because he is love*. This is what individuals impassioned for social justice are doing. They're executing wrath against sex-trafficking — including seeking "hell-on-earth" retribution for the traffickers — because it's truly loving to be utterly against great injustice for the sake of one's neighbor. Unfortunately for us, the greatest injustice ever perpetrated in the world was our rebellion against God. If I may paraphrase a "tweetable Puritan,"[28] there is no such thing as a minor sin, because there is no such thing as a minor God.

God's love. One of the biggest reasons we have cognitive dissonance (yeah, I took psychology in college) when it comes to God's wrath is because we have such a flat, unbiblical understanding of his love. Our view of God's love typically seems lifted from old scripts of *Love, American Style* or *The Love Boat* (any overly sentimentalized sitcom will do). Captain Stubing may not have had a wrath that "is revealed from heaven against all ungodliness and unrighteousness of men," but God does (see Romans 1:18). (Yes, my sitcom references need to be updated, but take it as a good sign that I've seen only half an episode of *Two and a Half Men*.)

The problem (about the love of God, not my sparse sitcom diet) is pointed out quite nicely by D.A. Carson in his little book, *The Difficult Doctrine of the Love of God*. In the book, Carson explains that we have taken one aspect of God's love and absolutized it. We say, "God is love," and somehow believe this pretty much sums it up, leaving us with a God about the size, shape, and jocularity of (here he comes again) Santa Claus. But as I've often said, God's attributes should always be seen together as a whole, not separately. God *is* love, but he is also just. Therefore his justice is loving. God *is* holy, but he is also love, so his love is holy, etc.

Most of the time, we don't even think about the many and varied aspects of God's love, and we handily ignore any verses about God hating sinners. What's even more troubling is that the fashionable evangelicals don't take much time to explain or define God's love in detail. They just seem to take their cues from the culture at large, which says: "Of course God loves me. Why wouldn't he? I'm wonderful. I could never love a God who doesn't love me. I could never love a God who would want to harm anyone."

This is pretty much the prevailing thinking of everyday American pagans who prefer a god just a few feet taller than they are. In trying to fold these people into the faith, some teachers, adopting the sentimentalized view of God's love, have reduced Jesus to the size of the average pagan, spiritually speaking. (Christianity itself doesn't have a height requirement.)

Professor of theology S. Lewis Johnson once said, "The Truth of God is not our Truth. It is God's Truth. When a man betrays the truthfulness of the Word of God over the false application of the principle of love, he is betraying God himself."[29] That is a strong accusation, but it applies to what is happening today with God's revealed love. The Word of God is being set aside for a one-dimensional, sentimentalized, human-centered view of love.

Does "Love" Demand Free Will?

This sentimental view of God's love, the one that sets forth a temporary hell, wants us to believe that God is so lovey-dovey he is able to melt every heart…he just can't melt every heart right now, in this life. And that's because, under this view, "love demands freedom."[30]

The claim behind this phrase is that if God were to *cause us* to love him in this life it would violate our free will, which means our love wouldn't be real. But look how it's worded: "Love demands freedom." Really? Because when you put it that way, it suggests that "love" is some kind of independent force. (What? Your Bible doesn't include the Book of Star Wars?)

"Love" is not a floaty cosmic being with its own mind and its own will. It is not an independent player on the scene. When I am faced with a significant moral decision, it would be good and right for me to consider what God thinks about the matter, as revealed in his Word. I might need to pray about it and perhaps seek advice from trusted Christian friends. But… "What would 'love' want me to do in this situation?" Take a question like that literally, and you're messing around in straight-up, old-school, the-crystals-have-powers paganism.

Whence doth come love, Romeo? The Bible (even more authoritative than Shakespeare) tells us that love is from God. Love is ultimately an attribute of God. It is not its own thing. You can *call* something "love," but to the extent that it is separated from the God who *is* love, it isn't really love at all. It's just a word. A word pointing to mere sentimentality and wishful thinking.

Christians often say things like "justice demands a sacrifice." What we mean is that God, in his justice, requires a sacrificial punishment for sin. We are (or should be) operating from a biblical definition of justice as an attribute of God. We don't (or shouldn't) put a spin on the meaning of *justice* simply because it suits our purposes. But when the nuovo hell teachers say "love demands freedom," they are really separating *love* from its biblical moorings and giving it a sentimental, humanistic spin.

So, a sentimental take on love might like to demand free will. But the love of God described in Scripture (the only perfect love there is) does not. So no, love doesn't actually do any demanding. God is the one who does the demanding. And he does not demand that, in order for our love for him to be real, our choice to love him must be made in complete freedom, without external compulsion. It's a distinction we shouldn't overlook if we want to avoid the evangellyfish[31] gospel.

In What Sense are People Free?

So the evangellyfish gospel would like to claim that if God influences our choice to love him, our love can't be real. The issue there is external influence. But what about internal influence? All on our own, completely apart from outside influences, are our choices completely free?

Consider for a moment that you were born into a specific environment within a specific family. You may have siblings, then later marry and have children. Professionally, you probably have an employer or employees. Add to this mix your own psychological glitches that all these fun relationships have helped you develop. Now, throw your own inclination toward selfishness into the blender. Puree for two minutes. And what do you get?

Radical depravity with pulp.

Every decision you make is tethered to a thousand (a million?) factors, each of them tied around your neck and pulling at you violently at the moment of choice.

Consider also the biblical teaching that our will is in bondage to sin. Put these elements together and it's clear that our freedom is far (really far) from absolute. You cannot sever your reactions or your decision-making from your influences, inclinations, and innate sinfulness. Even if love *could* demand freedom (in the external sense), it's clear we don't possess the kind of freedom (in the internal sense) suggested by the evangellyfish gospel. Our "freedom of the will" is closer to that of a man serving a life sentence for murder. Sure, he is still free…within the boundaries of the penitentiary.

Sorry, but if you're a Christian, I'm not offering you a way to pass the buck the next time you sin. The fact is that, for Christians, the issue of free will takes on some important nuances.

Christians start from the same baseline as non-Christians. First, we too are profoundly influenced by our own vast network of personal experiences and personality quirks. Second, despite these influences God is still sovereign over every moment of our lives, and we are still responsible for every choice we make. (Yes, both are true at the same time. It may be a hard concept for us to wrap our heads around, being that we're trying to wrap finite heads around the thoughts of an infinite God. This is why divine mystery always bends us toward humility. "Has not God made foolish the wisdom of the world?" [1 Corinthians 1:20]) The difference for Christians is that, at each and every decision point in this life there is available to us a response…a response we are capable of choosing by the power of the Holy Spirit…a response that pleases God and does not constitute sin (see 1 Corinthians 10:13). This is where, for example, the fruit of the Spirit comes into play, giving us the power to choose God's righteous alternative (see Galatians 5:22-24). In this sense, the Christian is much closer to being genuinely free than the non-Christian. Nevertheless, even for Christians, this is not even remotely the same thing as being actually, objectively free in the way that the convenient phrases of the free-will teachers suggest.

Only God is *that* free. Thankfully, he has exercised that freedom to make a way for us who are incapable of choosing him on our own. I love what Charles Spurgeon said, "Herein rests the power of the gospel. It does not ask your consent; but it gets it."[32]

God and Man — Who Loves First?

Where does the Bible come down on this idea that our love for God can only be genuine if we choose to love God out of our own free will?

Let's look at 1 John 4:10, for example: "In this is love, not that we have loved God…" Oopsie. We're off to a bad start here for the love-demands-freedom crowd. The Bible seems to be saying that love has to do with *God*, not with us.

In fact, to cut to the chase, the Bible teaches that we don't love God — in fact, in ourselves we hate him. (Need some backup on that? Check out Romans 3:10-18, 5:10; Ephesians 2:1-3; John 6:44; 1 John 4:19.) So if our hearts are naturally hostile toward God, does he have to wait until our hearts change before he grants us salvation? When do our hearts change, anyway?

- When we exercise faith?
- Make a decision?

We Lose the Love of God

- Raise a hand?
- Pray?
- Walk down the aisle?

Do *we* change our hearts? Or does God change our hearts?

When exactly does this happen?

As we think about the idea that for love to matter it has to include human free will, these are necessary and important questions.

Picking up 1 John 4:10, again…"In this is love, not that we have loved God but that he loved us and sent his Son to be the propitiation for our sins." We discussed propitiation briefly in chapter three. It means the satisfaction of God's wrath against sin, and it's really all about *consistency*. By which I mean this.

The death of Christ did not cause God to become loving. God was already loving. The satisfaction of his wrath against sin made it *consistent* for him to *show* us sinners his love.

It would be inconsistent for a holy God to overlook sin in his creatures. That's why he cannot let the guilty go unpunished. And that's why he has a wrath against all unrighteousness and why his wrath upholds the glory of his name. A God who would forgive us without the cross would be a very different God from the one we see in Scripture. The God of the Bible has a love that has nothing to do with vague-ish thoughts of infinite hugs. His love is fierce, holy, and wrathful. The love of God honors his holy character by displaying the only right reaction toward evil: wrath.

Propitiation reminds us that Jesus bears the blame

73

and the punishment for our sin—an option we could have never imagined, much less had the nerve to suggest. God takes the initiative in everything regarding our salvation. This is a gospel that doesn't need improvement, just clear proclamation, because it is some *good news*.

Whenever we talk about God's love we have to remember that, without the revelation of Scripture, we can easily become confused about what love really is. The corrupted version of divine love—the love expressed by fallen humanity—is often sentimental and selfish at its core. On the one hand, it is the unilateral, undeserved, initiating love of God that gives us the power and the reason to love people who don't love us. Yet as sinners, we manage to bring a measure of corruption into everything we do. To a great extent, therefore, we love people because of what they bring to our lives. We love them because of how they make us feel. We get something out of loving them. But God's love is never needy or sentimental. It has nothing in common with the kind of lovesick desperation that can't imagine being whole without the devotion of another. God does not love us because he needs us to love him back.

If we are to understand God's unilateral love, we have to push past all the "I'm so wonderful" self-esteem claptrap and recognize that in ourselves *there is nothing within us that provokes God's love*. His is a unilateral, saving love—a rescuing love. God demonstrated his own love toward us in that while we were yet sinners—those who rightfully deserve his wrath and hatred—he took action (Romans 5:8).

God loves us first, and he demonstrates his love. Christ is the demonstration.

God's Gospel Rescues

Let's go back to the story of Sunshine, the little girl who became a problem child after being abandoned by her mother. Do we say to her, "Be good, little girl, and then we'll love you. Become good and you can have a home." Is that what she needs? Do you think maybe her free will has been hindered by her experiences? Is her existing freedom of the will all she needs to know love? Or does she need to be rescued first to experience love?

We all know what Sunshine needs. She needs a family who will save her by embracing her with open arms. A family that says, "We will never leave you or forsake you." She could thrive in such an environment. She could begin to heal. She needs to be rescued from a status quo that is out of her control. She needs to be loved before she can love.

It's the same with each one of us. We need to be rescued by God who, by virtue of his Trinitarian nature, is family.

The love of God transforms us because it is not until we are born of God that we can love God. He changes the "environment" of our souls by giving us new hearts. He adopts us into his family. He promises to stand by our side always. God doesn't wait for our decision to love him, because that decision would never come. The truth is, we need his loving grace to come to us in a saving way *before* we can love him in return. We need his rescue mission.

This, of course, is radically different from the idea that love demands freedom—that for love to matter it must be "free." No, for love to matter it must be birthed from above by God himself.

"In this is love, not that we have loved God but that he loved us…"

God's Gospel Prevails

I admit it. At various points in this chapter, for the sake of argument, I've probably overemphasized God's sovereignty and downplayed human responsibility. But you know what? The Bible is full of tension between God's sovereign hand and our responsibility for our own conduct. You and I are certainly responsible for our choices, as the Bible shows, but God's plans are never overturned by human choice. "No purpose of yours can be thwarted" (Job 42:2). "All the inhabitants of the earth are accounted as nothing, and he does according to his will among the host of heaven and among the inhabitants of the earth; and none can stay his hand or say to him, 'What have you done?'" (Daniel 4:35).

This doesn't negate human responsibility. It just means that God's will prevails. The good he intends will come about, even when evil is planned against us, like in the case of Joseph whose brothers sold him into slavery (see Genesis 50:20).

It comes down to this: because of human bondage to sin, human choice alone is not enough. Humanity is spiritually dead and cannot become alive by an act of the will. "And you, who were dead in your trespasses and the uncircumcision of your flesh, God made alive together with him, having forgiven us all our trespasses" (Colossians 2:13).

Notice who made us alive.

The False Dichotomy: Frankenstein or Santa Claus

As an English Literature major in college, I took a course called "American Literature." As I recall, this is a rebellion against English Literature that protests by wasting tea. Anyway, the anthology to this course featured authors like Cotton Mather, Anne Bradstreet, Benjamin Franklin, Henry David Thoreau, Ralph Waldo Emerson, and five selected readings by the colonial preacher Jonathan Edwards.

Edwards' writings on nature alone are awe-inspiring for their depth, insight, and use of language. Either that or they just make you feel dumb. Usually both. But by far the most famous piece of writing from Edwards is his sermon, "Sinners in the Hands of an Angry God." I'd only been a Christian about a year when I took this course, and I was amazed that the professor had the entire class read it. It was like assigning the class a tract to read. I wondered if it was even legal. As I read that sermon, I couldn't help thinking, "This will get the whole class saved." I couldn't wait for the day we got to talk about it in class.

The day came, and I was astounded when not one classmate raised a hand and asked for prayer. I had the mistaken idea that coming to faith in Christ consisted of being given the right information about what to do. I thought that people gave you an explanation of the gospel and then you had the freedom to accept it or reject it. The terrifying images in this sermon only helped tilt you in the right direction. Or so I thought. But no one tilted. No one leaned. Basically, they yawned. "Sinners in the hands of an…" stretch with an arched back, arms extended while uttering Chewbacca-like sounds "…angry God."

Maybe the approach in that Edwards sermon was the problem. Instead of an angry God, maybe the whole class would've gotten saved if we'd read a sermon about a more approachable God. Then they would have somehow had the free will to choose Jesus. I should have sent a note to the professor.

No, I'm not saying the Edwards sermon is always and everywhere the best way to preach on hell. (Seriously. See Appendix B.) But some argue that if people don't respond to preaching on hell it's "because the God they've been presented with and taught about can't be loved. That God is terrifying and traumatizing and unbearable."[33] Sure he is, when presented as a one-dimensional caricature, a Frankenstein God who's basically just out to throttle you.

But hold on a minute. The preachers of the evangelly-fish gospel claim that people *can* be provoked to respond unilaterally to a Santa Claus God of love and mercy. If so, then why couldn't people at least sometimes be provoked to respond unilaterally to a God of holiness and wrath against sin? If you would respond on your own to a lovey-dovey God to gain love, why wouldn't you respond on your own to a Frankenstein God to get rid of fear? You'd think some people would respond just to stop their knees from knocking. But they don't.

The fact is, we don't respond unilaterally to either one. First, because neither one is God to begin with—that's right, the Frankenstein/Santa Claus dichotomy is a farce and a false choice. But more importantly, we don't respond unilaterally because we *can't*.

God uses *his* truth (not our new-and-improved caricatures) as the means by which he reaches people. We must therefore use the comprehensive truth of who God is as the means of reaching people—not just those parts of the truth that we think we can manipulate to achieve greater effectiveness. Manipulation is manipulation, whether we use fear or love as the means.

In the crucifixion of Jesus, we find neither the Frankenstein God nor the Santa Claus God. We find the God who is, a God of love *and* wrath, of mercy *and* justice. At the cross, we realize that God's love and God's wrath are not only compatible, but they embrace. In the death and resurrection of Jesus, God maintains his justice, upholds his holiness, and shows us mercy by redirecting his wrath from us to his Son, because of his great love for us. In the cross of Jesus Christ, God's love and God's wrath embrace in a display of his holy nature before the entire universe, leaving angels in awe and demons dumbfounded.

I have to confess that, even now, it doesn't feel encouraging to write about such a negative subject as hell. But in keeping with the promise of this book's title, here near the end of the book I'd like to offer an encouraging note: I'd like to encourage you to not go to hell.

Instead, believe in Christ.

Afterword
THE WORST FUNERAL EVER
Not That the Sandwiches Weren't Delicious

Most preachers have a good funeral story, and a bad funeral story. Rob Bell is no exception. Bell tells one of those "friend of a friend" bad funeral stories in his book, *Love Wins*.[34] It goes something like this: A young man was killed in a car accident. The young man's sister was asked by someone, "Was he a Christian?" The sister replied, "No, he was an atheist." The person then said, "So there's no hope, then."

Bell finds it incredible that a confirmed atheist would be considered lost in the afterlife. "Is this the Christian message? No hope?" he keeps asking. (Actually, if everyone eventually goes to heaven, then I guess there's no such thing as a bad funeral story.)

Here is something many preachers think but rarely verbalize: *the eternal destinies of some are more obvious than others.* We think this because the Bible makes the case for it. (See 1 John, the entire letter.) Honestly, there are a lot of things the Bible teaches that Christians are afraid to say out loud. But the Bible never does what we often do in the Christian community—it never sweeps the theological dirt under the rug, or even under an embarrassing evangelist's hairpiece. We usually stay silent, for example, about Old Testament genocide and the passages where Jesus warns plainly of eternal punishment. You might want to say we're just looking out for God's reputation, but…really? God didn't ask us to run interference for him. My guess is it's our own reputation we're most worried about. ("You people believe *what??*")

Anyway, the Bible teaches that our eternal destinies are hinted at by the path we're on. These are not thoughts we like to utter, because every Christian knows someone whose spiritual state is suspect, like the old high-school buddy lying in a casket who, thanks to his snickering pals, now has a joint in his right hand and a forty-ouncer under his left. Our lives leave trails that indicate which road we're on, and there are really only two—the broad road that leads to destruction or the narrow road that leads to life. (Pardon me for writing with conviction.)

My mother died a few months ago, so this issue has true emotional force for me—it's not just abstract theological doctrine or intellectual gymnastics. Nobody wants to speak ill about a parent's wake, but my mother's was the most pathetic event I've ever attended. I don't mean pathetic in the sense of sad. Sure it was sad. It was just somehow a very uneventful event.

They called it a wake. Okay. It definitely wasn't a funeral, because there was no service. *Visitation* just sounds moronic—you don't visit dead people. And I guess you can't call it a gathering for the dead.

Still, *wake* implies some type of vigil. But there wasn't even a vigil. It was more like:

"Mom died."

"Oh, um…well, let's order Subway."

We only expected a handful of people, which is also sad, but around twenty showed up. There we were: my sister and her family, me and my family, a handful of other relatives and acquaintances, eating select meats and breads with a photo of my mother in the room. That was it. Show up, say hello to some folks you hardly know, others you see maybe once a year, pick out a cookie and chips to go with your meal, and go about your life. Maybe it would have been different if we had all told heartwarming stories about my mother. But no one did. Just polite conversation and cold cuts.

My sister asked if I wanted to say a few words, but I truly didn't know what to say. "The sandwiches are delicious?" I hadn't planned anything. I can usually speak extemporaneously (and for extended periods of time as those who've been cornered by me at Starbucks can attest), but words at a Subway-catered mourning should be carefully planned.

I had prayed for several years that God would give me assurance of my mother's salvation. I'd spoken with her about the gospel for years. I regretted not talking about it more. During some of our conversations she seemed to have faith in Christ and at other times she seemed tossed about by every wind of doctrine as seen on Oprah. I never saw convincing fruit in her life.

When I was a kid, my mother periodically rotated through several stories about how German fortune tellers and psychics had predicted her future. She insisted that everything they said to her had come true. Except the part about becoming rich. That part never panned out. My nieces mentioned they'd heard the same stories from her. It saddens me that she didn't tell any stories of how Jesus changed her life.

My sister told me that, a week or so before Mom died, she said, "Why won't God take me?"

"I dunno, Mom," my sister answered.

Then my mother said some revealing words, "Maybe he doesn't want me."

Certainly, a believer can die without assurance of salvation and find oneself in God's presence. Conversely, a professing believer can die with what feels like assurance of salvation and end up in hell. That's why the apostle John went to great lengths in his letters to give signposts so we can rightly judge ourselves and our fruit.

It's sad for a Christian to die without assurance of salvation, but it's not a tragedy. Still, how many years can a person remain a baby Christian? Can a person actually be a Christian for years without ever growing and maturing? Don't let your friends and loved ones be plagued with these questions after you die. The Bible tells us that Christians should not mourn death like other people (see 1 Thessalonians 4:13). Christians who lose a saved friend or loved one should be able to have joy in the grief.

Make sure your life leaves some evidence of your relationship with Christ. It will make the sandwiches more enjoyable.

My mother feared God but was uncertain of being accepted by him. When I wonder if I'll see my mom in heaven, I can't answer for certain. All I know is that the Judge of all the earth will do right.

This raises a question that's often asked about loved ones who do not follow Christ. People want to know how it's possible to enjoy heaven when a family member or close friend is suffering endless punishment in hell. Most of us have experienced some form of physical torment and can't even begin to imagine it lasting forever.

Last month I suffered from a virus that plagued the left side of my head and my left inner ear. I was in debilitating pain. I didn't want to eat or even watch television. That's how bad it was—I couldn't even stare. This lasted two weeks. I went to the hospital twice. And I learned a lot about morphine. Mainly that it doesn't last very long. (It's hard to be a drug addict.)

While lying in bed, writhing in pain, intermittently rocking from side to side, I thought of hell. I thought to myself, "I can't imagine this lasting forever. This is torment."

This question—about the awareness of dead relatives in hell putting a damper on our heavenly joy—is most commonly answered these days with, "I don't know. It's a mystery as deep and wide as our faith." There's certainly some truth to that answer. Our faith is deep and wide, and we will never fully comprehend an incomprehensible God. It's absolutely impossible for the finite to take in the infinite. But we don't walk in complete ignorance. The simple premise of Christianity is that the only way we can know anything about the infinite, personal God of the universe is if he reveals himself to us. Christianity contends that God revealed aspects of himself to humanity, first through the law and prophets and then through his Son. Thus, while it's true we can't understand *everything* about heaven, this doesn't mean we can't understand *something* about it.

Jesus said, "If anyone comes to me and does not

hate his own father and mother and wife and children and brothers and sisters, yes, and even his own life, he cannot be my disciple" (Luke 14:26). Sure, there's some hyperbole there, but it's hyperbole in the service of an underlying point—compared to our love and devotion to God, the love and devotion we have for our loved ones, even our own lives, will seem like hate. This may be easy to apply to how you feel about your mother-in-law, but it's meant for more.

There is one person alone who will make heaven (the new earth) matter, and that is the person of God. In the presence of God no one else will truly matter. This offends our modern sensibilities because we make much of ourselves and little of God. Sometimes we assume we'll be able to continue with such shallow thinking in the next life. To be blunt, however, having our loved ones around is not what will make heaven heavenly. Sure, we'd be thrilled to see them, but let's be honest. Most of us can barely sit through a Thanksgiving dinner with some of our closest relatives, yet somehow we think heaven won't really be enjoyable unless they're with us. Look, there are days I can barely stand myself. And if you're honest, you've had those days, too, when you can barely stand me, either.

It is God alone who will make heaven glorious.

As for the idea, floated by some of the nuovo hell teachers, that it wouldn't be fair to leave folks in hell now that they see the error of their ways and are newly repentant…well, this assumes that people in hell *will* be repentant. That may not be the case. There is the idea seen in Scripture that on this earth the Spirit of God presently restrains the sins of humanity (2 Thessalonians 2:7). That means, as bad as we are, we could be a lot worse.

"So, you're tellin' me that Stalin was restrained?"

Yeah.

Imagine Stalin unrestrained.

In hell God will withdraw all the positive restraint of his Spirit. This means that in hell people will become even more bitter and angry and idolatrous. People won't be repentant in hell. They will become more impenitent. People will hate God even more in hell than they did on earth.

Let me offer a down-to-earth example to the objection that you won't be able to enjoy heaven if you know some of your friends or loved ones are in hell. Say you have an uncle who, in the process of carjacking a family's car, ends up killing both parents, leaving two young children as orphans. Are you going to be sad that his sentencing calls for prison time? Even if he was your favorite uncle, I know you would have compassion on the children he orphaned, and I'm pretty sure you'd acknowledge that his being in prison is just. Even though he's your uncle, you can't deny that he deserves what he's getting.

When we get to heaven, and are in the presence of God's absolute holy perfection, we will for the first time truly see sin for what it is—crimes against the infinite, personal, and holy God of the universe. Our love, devotion, and loyalty toward God himself will completely overwhelm the attachments we had here on earth. So, as hard as it might be to imagine now, we won't be grieved at all if our favorite uncle is in hell. Instead, we will see his punishment for what it is—we will see that it is just.

This was the view of the intellectual Puritan, Jonathan Edwards. He believed that the redeemed would actually witness the torment of the damned. Since the Bible declares that "the smoke of their torment" continually rises up before the angels and the presence of the Lamb (Revelation 14:11), Edwards assumed the saints would witness it, too. But if that's true, seeing the smoke won't be a source of grief. Just the opposite. It will elicit praise for the grace God has shown to the redeemed in Christ. Their misery without end will, by contrast, magnify the glory of heaven.

Whether by heaven or by hell, God will be glorified in every life.

We were not born for infinite happiness. We were born to glorify God. And one can either do that in heaven or in hell.

> Has the potter no right over the clay, to make out of the same lump one vessel for honorable use and another for dishonorable use? What if God, desiring to show his wrath and to make known his power, has endured with much patience vessels of wrath prepared for destruction, in order to make known the riches of his glory for vessels of mercy, which he has prepared beforehand for glory (Romans 9:21–23).

The person in Bell's funeral story who said, "So there's no hope," brought up some literally vital biblical concepts.

> It is appointed for man to die once, and after that comes judgment (Hebrews 9:27).

> You will recognize them by their fruits (Matthew 7:16).

> Now the works of the flesh are evident: sexual immo-
> rality, impurity, sensuality, idolatry, sorcery, enmity,
> strife, jealousy, fits of anger, rivalries, dissensions,
> divisions, envy, drunkenness, orgies, and things like
> these. I warn you, as I warned you before, that those
> who do such things will not inherit the kingdom of
> God (Galatians 5:19–21).

To summarize these vital ideas: *after* we die we are
judged, and *before* we die there are markers that can give
a pretty good indication of which road we're on. That's
right, loving God will always influence how we live. If it
doesn't…well, that's serious business. The Bible repeatedly tells us there is a direct link between how we live our
lives and how much we love God.

The Bible never contends that people are *saved* by
how they live; we are saved by grace alone. But the gospel
of grace is about more than putting us in right standing
with God—it is also about the regenerating power of the
Holy Spirit who gives us new hearts, by which we live a
different sort of life than we had prior to our conversion.

From the perspective of finite and fallible humans,
there are certainly gray areas in this matter of fruits and
salvation. Only God truly knows someone's heart. Some
people look at this and conclude that we should never
speculate on the eternal destinies of others.

Hmm.

Then why would Jesus say, "Bear fruit in keeping
with repentance" (Matthew 3:8)? Why would he tell
about the sheep and the goats in Matthew 25, where the
difference between them was what they did? Why would
he say in Matthew 7:15-20 that different kinds of people

bear different kinds of fruit in their lives? These passages have to mean that Christians have a certain quality to their lives, a certain type of fruit.

There *are* indications about which path someone is on. And we are called to use those indications either to encourage one another in the faith or to express our concern.

If you've spent much time around evangelicals, you probably know strong believers and weak believers, people who seem to display a maturity beyond their years in the faith and others who say they love Jesus but struggle year after year with the same significant sin issues. It's that second group that's really troubling, professing Christians who have little understanding and little fruit. These are the hard cases, the ones where eternal destinies are less obvious because the people involved are Good Joes. The Rotten Joes are much more obvious, and when you know people really well, it's easier to pick out which of your friends are probably going to hell (since living like hell often has something to do with being on our way to hell).

Don't be misled into thinking that only pagans, whores, politicians, and comedians end up in hell. Hell will be full of respectable people, Good Joes, like school teachers and doctors and nurses and firemen. Churchgoers, even.

So if we want to line up with Scripture on this question, we *have to* use the "fruits" measurement to help us determine who is in the faith and who isn't. If you believe in a biblical hell—a yes or no for all eternity—then you must be willing to warn those whose lives cause you concern. To not do this is cruel.

And encouraging people to believe in a second-chance or temporary hell? That's more than cruel. It's heretical, despicable, and cruel.

How (seriously…*how*?) could any preacher equipped with low to medium biblical knowledge think you shouldn't tell a practicing atheist—someone actively engaged in the business of not-believing—that his eternal soul is in a precarious state unless he repents and believes the gospel? Paul was driven to tears as he pleaded with people (see 2 Corinthians 2:4, Philippians 3:18). We should do the same. (Right there, we show love to the sinner even as we hate the sin, all in the same breath.) But a gospel defanged of hell doesn't need to weep, plead, or pray. If the atheist is happy and doesn't want to follow Jesus, well, no big deal…there's still hope. "We'll get you in the next life!"

The revisionist view of the afterlife treats sin with kid gloves. It gives people who have no hope a false hope that they can come to Jesus anytime—now, later, sometime after you die, when you feel like it, doesn't matter very much…it's all good.

Look, I'm sorry, but that's a message of damnation. It's not the gospel. It's not from the Bible. It's a hellish lie.

This is the warning Jesus gives to those who lead Christians to sin. "Whoever causes one of these little ones who believe in me to sin, it would be better for him…" (We interrupt this quotation to observe that, at this point Jesus could have said a lot of things, and apparently he chose what follows as the best available option.) "…if a great millstone were hung around his neck and he were thrown into the sea" (Mark 9:42). That's right: head stuck into the hole of a giant stone doughnut. Hurtling to the bottom of the ocean. Neck first. That would be *better* than the best-case scenario for the unbeliever who leads Christians to sin. I don't even want to think of what awaits those who lead people to an eternal hell by giving them false hope with a false gospel. Probably a *worse* eternal hell, one hell of a hell.

This is what baffles me the most about these old heresies made new. If my view of eternal punishment turns out to be wrong, then I'll be surprised and delighted upon entering the afterlife. "Hey, look, it's my favorite uncle from prison!" But if you die dis-believing the saving gospel and die believing you'll have another chance… what happens then if you're wrong? Not only is there no purgatorial bus ride. You will have missed the bus, period. All hope gone forever.

Recently, after a program in Rocky Mount, Virginia, I was talking to a man by the name of Karl Schad whose mother had also recently died. She had been in a coma and was expected to die, but she just kept hanging on. One of the nurses asked him, "Is everyone here?"

Karl said, "I don't understand."

"They often hold on to say goodbye to someone who hasn't arrived yet," the nurse explained. "I see it all the time."

Karl said, "Her sister from Florida, but she isn't coming."

"Then tell her," said the nurse.

So Karl leaned over and told his mother that she didn't need to wait because her sister wasn't going to be able to make it. "But she wanted me to tell you that she loves you," he whispered.

Within half an hour, she passed.

The nurse was convinced that dying people in comas can hear us. There is no medical proof of this, as far as I know. Still, I was strangely moved by Karl's tale, because I had so often prayed that the Lord would give me assurance of my mother's salvation and somehow let me know that she was in his loving presence when she left this world. Even after she died, I continued praying this prayer, finally taking the unanswered prayer as a bad sign.

So I stopped asking about it.

Then a few weeks later I talked to Karl and thought to myself, "This could be the answer." As always, I expected a more extraordinary answer to my prayer, something like a vision or a dream, my mother in a white choir robe waving at me, saying, "It's okay. I'm with the Lord."

I hope this simple conversation with Karl was it.

Before my mother passed away, my sister held the phone up to my mother's ear, and I passionately told her one last time about trusting Christ, stressing that it is by grace we are saved through faith in what he has done for us by dying on the cross and rising again from the dead. I can't remember my exact words, but I remember hoping that she could somehow hear me. After hearing Karl's story, I now hold out hope that she did hear me and I will see her one day in paradise. Even if she's living next to the thief on the cross, it doesn't matter because there are no bad neighborhoods in heaven.

Still, if you happen to be a professing Christian, leave your family some evidence.

This past summer I went to family camp with my wife and kids—a week of walking too much, eating too much, and getting bitten by bugs long thought to be extinct. At family camp my wife and I met another

Christian couple. Somehow the topic of death came up as it often does on such vacations. (Maybe someone had a lingering fear of being eaten by a bear?) The young lady explained to my wife and me that her father was radically saved when she was 1 year old. Her dad was a former drug dealer whose father was the Northwest leader of the Hell's Angels. (I didn't even know they *had* regional supervisors). Her relatives still have large cherry farms that are just fronts where they grow acres of pot. Anyway, her dad was converted and began the life of an evangelist. Evangelism was his passion but never his source of income. When his daughter was 12, he died of stomach cancer. His wife said to his then 12-year-old daughter, "Maybe we should put something in the paper. Every week he talked about so-and-so who got saved. It always seemed to be somebody." So she put a little something in the paper about his funeral and 2,500 people showed up to honor this man who touched their lives with the gospel of Christ.

Our lives will leave some evidence of our eternal destinies.

May we all have such encouraging funerals.

Have a good death.

And prepare for it courageously.

Appendix A
A IS FOR ANNIHI-
LATIONISM

And for Assigning the Burden of Poof

Jesus didn't speak of hell in a way that made it less frightening. Instead, he made it more frightening. Using the Old Testament teaching on Sheol, he expanded our understanding of it by showing us an even more fearful picture of eternal misery. This is why I'm a little perplexed by how much credibility is given to the idea of annihilationism, a heterodox view of hell which declares God will punish you for a time, just to make a point, and then obliterate you, so you won't remember his point. Thus, *ouch* and *poof*—you will no longer exist. Annihilationists have a hard time making their position frightening, because according to their view, God is saying, "I'm going to teach you a lesson that you will soon forget."

Okay. Whatever.

This view of hell amounts to no hell, because a hell you can't remember is no hell.

The other problem with annihilationism is the Bible—specifically those passages that clearly teach eternal conscious punishment (Luke 16:19–31; Matthew

13:41-42, 49-50; Matthew 24:50-51; Matthew 22:13; Matthew 18:34-35; Matthew 25:30; 2 Thessalonians 1:5–9; Jude 13). But annihilationists like to point to passages of Scripture that use the word *destruction* when speaking about someone's fate. How can we harmonize the destruction passages with the eternal conscious punishment passages? It's a valid question.

I happen to believe that God gave us a Bible that allows normal people with normal lives to understand its essential message with all the clarity they need. And this whole business about whether hell is permanent or temporary? That strikes me as pretty essential, so I believe there's enough clarity for us right there in the plain words of Scripture.

This may seem like an odd place to start when considering whether the Bible teaches annihilationism, but let's consider where Jesus said of Judas, "It would have been better for that man if he had not been born" (Matthew 26:24). Jesus is saying that for Judas, non-existence —having never existed at all—would be better than something else. What was this something else?

- Is non-existence better for someone than an eternity in heaven? *Wait…let me think…No.*
- Is non-existence better for someone than an eternity in hell? *Definitely. Yes.*

So Jesus is clearly saying Judas is on his way to hell. But from the perspective of annihilationism the question then becomes:

- Is non-existence better for someone than an eternity of non-existence? *Huh?*

If annihilationism is true, then what Jesus said here about Judas is pretty much nonsense, or at least so weak as to be nearly meaningless. It's a throwaway statement, the kind of stuff people politely ignore at parties because it doesn't really add anything to the conversation. And if annihilationism is true, then what Jesus said about Judas could be said about every person who goes to hell.

Why not trot this out at a party sometime? See how it goes.

"As an annihilationist, I agree with Jesus that nonexistence is better than nonexistence."

"Uh-huh. What's in the dip? As an annihilationist, I hope you understand why this conversation is over."

Jesus wasn't given to nonsense or throwaway statements. His every word mattered deeply. A permanent hell is the only context that gives his statement any real force or meaning. If annihilationism is true, then at this point in his ministry Jesus was basically just babbling. And he didn't do that.

Given all this, what *does* the Bible mean when it says, for example, in 2 Thessalonians 1:9, that the unbelieving "will suffer the punishment of eternal destruction"? Not to beat an eternally dead horse, but when you read one of these "destruction" passages, just imagine someone leaning over and whispering in your ear, "It would have been better for them if they had not been born." Then, remember that the only option that gives this "not been born" phrase any force is a hell of eternally conscious punishment. Because "nonexistence is better than nonexistence" just doesn't work.

But I actually do have a second point.

Remember how God told Adam and Eve in Genesis

3 that they would die if they ate of the tree? Well, in a sense they didn't. That is, their bodies did not physically die at that moment. But they did die spiritually, and they knew it. That's why they were guiltily trying to hide from God. They knew that something very serious had happened, that something had changed in their relationship with God. They had suffered death spiritually and would now eventually suffer it physically. This was the destruction of hope and of peace with God. It was the destruction of joy and of gladness and of a meaningful existence. It was the eternal destruction of spiritual death.

Thankfully, God quickly held out the promise of salvation, the possibility of escape from this death and destruction. But for those who do not experience God's salvation, the sentence placed upon Adam and Eve remains.

The New Testament references to destruction refer to a spiritual destruction, just like the spiritual death experienced by Adam and Eve in the Garden. This destruction represents the loss of all hope, all joy, all chance of reconciliation. It is truly a destruction that lasts forever.

Seen this way, the "destruction" verses align perfectly with the "eternal conscious punishment" verses. It's not those who believe in the traditional hell who need to defend their interpretation of the "eternal" passages. It's the annihilationists who need to defend their interpretation of the "destruction" passages. Call it the burden of poof.

Besides, why would Jesus have said "eternal punishment" if he actually meant "really bad but technically temporary punishment"? These passages are clearly about the afterlife. Yet Jesus didn't say, "And these will go away into God's Big Time Out. But the righteous to eternal life."

If annihilationism is true, why did Jesus choose such misleading phrases?

When I was a kid I used to hide to the side of a hallway in our home and when my mother came walking down the hall I'd make a clawing motion and roar. She would jump, scream, and get really mad. The madder she became the more I couldn't help laughing. And the more I laughed, the madder she became.

When you scare someone and they get angry, unfortunately, it is funny, but I can't begin to ascribe such motives to the Son of God (not that he didn't have a sense of humor, being the creator of humor and all). Why would he want to scare us by calling it eternal damnation if it's really only temporary?

Jesus would never warn us about an eternal hell if it wasn't a legitimate warning.

Our difficulty with the New Testament's teaching on eternal punishment doesn't have to do with understanding the verses. It has to do with our emotional reaction to them. I hope. Otherwise it's much worse, as in suppressing the truth because of unrighteousness (Romans 1:18).

The truth is, Jesus made hell even more frightening.

A WORD TO PASTORS ABOUT PREACHING THE DOCTRINE OF HELL

Do it Regularly, Clearly, and with Tears

The current cultural status quo simply laughs off the doctrine of hell. If that's ever going to change, it's going to have to happen in part through you, the local pastor. Here are five ways you can help overturn this cultural mindset.

1. You must preach on hell unashamedly, forcefully, and with tears. You'll find that your confidence in declaring these truths grows as you declare them because they *are* true and carry the weight of God's authority.
2. Preach on it more often than you have in the past. (How many sermons did you preach just on hell alone in the past year?) Become part of the new breed of hellfire-and-brimstone preachers. Start planning

your yearly sermon series on eternal punishment now. But you don't have to limit it to one series per year on the subject. It's a more versatile subject than you can imagine. If you need brainstorming assistance, consider this your own personal launchpad. What are we launching? A hurricane of ideas! You can do a series on "What Jesus Said about Damnation," and just focus on Christ's words on the subject. Call it "Red Words about Hell." You can do an overview, following the doctrine from the Old to the New Testament: "Hell through the Ages" or "Hell from a Distance." You can do a series that harmonizes God's love with God's wrath: "The Frankenstein/Santa Claus False Dichotomy." You can contrast two street-level objections such as "Is it fair for God to punish people eternally?" with "Is it fair for God to reward people eternally?" Just open the Book and preach on the reality of the next life: "Why Hell Won't Make Heaven Bittersweet." Etc., etc., etc.

3. Don't assume everyone in your congregation of professing Christians is saved. Preach so as to convert even the elect! "Depart from me, I never knew you," is going to be said to people who claimed they knew him (Matthew 7:23).

4. Believe that God wants to save people through your ministry. The most encouraging thing of all is that God wants to save people by the foolishness of our preaching his powerful gospel.

5. Eternal punishment is part of the gospel and should be included when we present the gospel. The gospel is about justifying God. That is, it's about how he

can save us from what we deserve and still remain just. Hold up high the greatness of God, and the Holy Spirit will do the work of convicting people of what their sin deserves. It's not about scaring people. It's about preaching the reality of God's character! Preach the Word of God with conviction, like you will one day stand before the judgment seat of Christ. Because you will. We all will.

Acknowledgements

Writing is always more of a community endeavor than most realize, so there are always people to thank:

Marshall Allen, agent and editor, as always you are indispensable in every way, from inception to completion.

Kevin Meath, Bob Bevington, and everyone at Cruciform Press for being men of their word and for publishing this work. God is glorified by the way you conduct your business.

The people of Canyon Lake Community Church in general and the Threshold service in particular for being thirsty people. You all make preaching a pleasure, aside from that one guy in the second row who frowns a lot.

Pastors Pete Van Dyke, Dave Dick and Bryan Pitotti for being men who accept me even as Christ has accepted me. Leading with you all has been one of my life's greatest privileges.

Pastor Forrest Short, if not for your generous leadership I wouldn't be preaching today. (So really, it's all your fault.)

My wife, Dinika, who becomes more dear to me with each passing day. We have a truly gospel-blessed marriage.

My daughters, Eden Olivia and Kate Tulip, I hope you both read this one day with a love for Jesus as the Truth. (Don't worry. I'll save you a copy.)

Endnotes

1. George M. Marsden, *Jonathan Edwards: A Life* (New Haven, CT: Yale University Press, 2004) p 457
2. Rob Bell, *Love Wins* (San Francisco: HarperOne, 2010), p viii
3. Christopher W. Morgan and Robert A. Peterson, *Hell Under Fire* (Grand Rapids: Zondervan, 2004), p 40
4. John Stott, quoted in James I. Packer, "Evangelical Annihilationism in Review." Reformation & Revival, 6:2 (Spring 1997), http://www.biblicalstudies.org.uk/pdf/ref-rev/06-2/6-2_packer.pdf (Accessed December 5, 2013)
5. Robert Farrar Capon seems to espouse this view in his trilogy *Kingdom, Grace, Judgment* (Grand Rapids: Eerdmans, 2002). To be fair, Capon's view affirms all are saved in Jesus Christ alone, and he seems to affirm hell in one form or another (p 269), but only after much qualification.
6. Brian McLaren, *The Last Word and the Word After That* (San Francisco: Jossey-Bass, 2008), p 103
7. David Lloyd, *The Mary Tyler Moore Show*, "Chuckles Bites the Dust," episode 7, season 6
8. Jerry Bridges, *The Joy of Fearing God* (Colorado Springs: WaterBrook Press, 1997), p 2
9. Loraine Boettner, *Reformed Doctrine of Predestination* (Phillipsburg, NJ: The Presbyterian and Reformed Publishing Company, 1980), p 71, Kindle Edition
10. Timothy J. Keller, "The Dark Garden," preached April 2, 2000. http://str.typepad.com/weblog/2013/04/page/3/ (Accessed December 18, 2013)
11. P.J. Achtemeier, ed., *Harper's Bible Dictionary*, 1st ed. (San Francisco: Harper & Row, 1985), p 646
12. R.C. Sproul, *The Holiness of God* (Carol Stream, IL: Tyndale House Publishers, 1998), p 38
13. Sam Storms, "The Holiness of God," blog entry May 22, 2006, http://www.samstorms.com/all-articles/post/the-holiness-of-god (Accessed December 18, 2013)
14. R.C. Sproul, *The Holiness of God* (Carol Stream, IL: Tyndale House Publishers, 1998), p 39
15. Mark Driscoll, *Doctrine: What Christians Should Believe* (Wheaton, IL: Crossway, 2010), p 259
16. Richard Owen Roberts, *Repentance: The First Word of the Gospel* (Wheaton, IL: Crossway, 2002), p 72

17. John Frame, *The Doctrine of God* (Phillipsburg, NJ: P & R Publishing, 2002), p. 461

18. Ibid., p 79

19. J.I. Packer, *Knowing God* (Downers Grove, IL: InterVarsity Press, 1973), p 130

20. Stuart Townend, "How Deep the Father's Love," Kingsway's Thankyou Music, 1995

21. *NIV Study Bible, 10th Anniversary Edition* (Grand Rapids, MI: Zondervan, 1995)

22. To be clear, unbelief is not the reason people are condemned. They are condemned because they are sinners.

23. The belief that people suffer in hell for a period of time but are then obliterated into nonexistence. This will be explained in further detail in Appendix A.

24. This story was modified from a story that Tim Keller once told.

25. Read: Christ as example.

26. Bill Hicks, *Rants in E Minor* (Arizona Bay Production Co., 1997), track 27, "Christianity"

27. Bell, back cover, First Edition

28. "Tweetable Puritans" comes from http://www.challies.com/reading-classics-together/satan-wants-to-help-you (accessed December 7, 2013). The original quote is "There is no little sin, because no little God to sin against," from *Precious Remedies Against Satan's Devices*, by Thomas Brooks.

29. S. Lewis Johnson, "Unchanging Truth of the Gospel: Galatians" http://sljinstitute.net/sermons/new%20testament/pauls/pages/galatians4.html (Accessed December 18, 2013.)

30. Bell, p 113

31. Douglas Wilson coined this most useful term in his novel, *Evangellyfish*.

32. Iain H. Murray, The Forgotten Spurgeon, (Carlisle, PA: Banner of Truth Trust, 1966), p 99

33. Bell, pp 174-175

34. Bell, p 3

Smooth Stones

Bringing Down the Giant
Questions of Apologetics

by Joe Coffey

**Street-level apologetics for
everyday Christians.**

**Because faith in Jesus makes
sense. And you don't need
an advanced degree
to understand why.**

101 pages   bit.ly/CPStones

"What a thrill for me to see Joe Coffey, a graduate of our first Centurions
Program class, apply the biblical worldview principles we teach at
BreakPoint and the Colson Center. In this marvelous little book, Joe
simply and succinctly lays out the tenets of the Christian faith within
the context of the four key life and worldview questions. This is an
excellent resource for Christians and non-Christians alike who are
seeking the Truth."
>   ***Chuck Colson, Founder of Prison Fellowship and the Colson
>   Center for Christian Worldview***

"This book may be the best resource I've seen to answer common
objections in everyday language."
>   ***Jared Totten, Critical Thinking Blog***

"A quick read that packs a punch .... I'm always on the lookout for
something like this. *Smooth Stones* is a winner. "
>   ***Mike del Rosario, ApologeticsGuy.Com***

"Most books on apologetics are too long, too deep, and too complicat-
ed. This book has none of these defects. Like its title, it is like a smooth
stone from David's apologetic sling directed right to the mind of an
enquiring reader"
>   ***Norman L. Geisler, Distinguished Professor of Apologetics,
>   Veritas Evangelical Seminary, Murrieta, CA***

Good News About Satan
A Gospel Look at Spiritual Warfare

by Bob Bevington
Foreword by Jerry Bridges

The world, the flesh...the Devil and his demons. How do they work together against us?

Learn to recognize and resist the enemy in the power of the gospel.

108 pages
bit.ly/SATANLOSES

"Spiritual warfare is certainly an important biblical topic; from one perspective it is the central topic of the whole Bible. So it's important that believers get sober and reliable guidance on the subject. Bob Bevington's book is one of the most helpful. His book is reliable, biblical, and practical. It is easy to understand and challenges our spiritual complacency."

Dr. John M. Frame, Reformed Theological Seminary

"This is the best book I have ever read on this subject. I simply could not put it down. It is both highly Christ-centered and very practical, having the wonderful effect of focusing the reader's attention directly on Jesus while at the same time providing much useful help in the believer's battle against the enemy."

Mike Cleveland, Founder and President, Setting Captives Free

"Filled with biblical reconnaissance and helpful insights for the conduct of spiritual warfare... a stimulating analysis of the biblical data, drawing boundaries between the factual and fanciful, and grounding the reader firmly on the gospel of Jesus Christ."

Stanley Gale, author, What is Spiritual Warfare?

"Read this book, prepare for battle, and rejoice in the victory that has been won and the glory that will shine more brightly."

Justin Taylor, co-author, The Final Days of Jesus

Inductive Bible Studies for Women by Keri Folmar

Endorsed by Kathleen Nielson, Diane Schreiner,
Connie Dever, Kristie Anyabwile, Gloria Furman

JOY! – A Bible Study on Philippians for Women	GRACE: A Bible Study on Ephesians for Women	FAITH: A Bible Study on James for Women
A 10-week study	*A 10-week study*	*A 10-week study*

A Bible Study for Women on the Gospel of Mark

SON OF GOD Volume 1	SON OF GOD Volume 2
An 11-week study	*An 11-week study*

"It is hard to imagine a better inductive Bible Study tool."
–Diane Schreiner

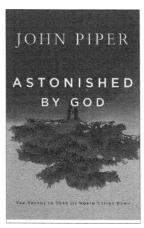

Astonished by God
Ten Truths to Turn the World Upside Down

by John Piper

Turn your world on its head.

192 pages

Published for Desiring God by Cruciform Press

bit.ly/AstonishedbyGod

For more than thirty years, John Piper pastored in the rough and tumble realities of downtown Minneapolis, preaching his people through the ups and down of life one Sunday at a time. When it came to capturing a generation of joy in one final sermon series, he turned to ten trademark truths to leave ringing in his peoples' ears.

These ten are world-shaking truths—each astonishing in its own way. First they turned Piper's own world upside down. Then his church's. And they will continue to turn the whole world upside down as the gospel of Christ advances in distance and depth. These surprising doctrines, as Piper writes, are "wildly untamable, explosively uncontainable, and electrically future-creating."

Join a veteran author, pastor, and Christian statesman as he captures the ten astonishing, compassionate, life-giving, joy-awakening, hope-sustaining truths that have held everything together for him.

The Joy Project
An Introdction to Calvinism

by Tony Reinke

**True happiness is not found.
It finds you.**

*Published for Desiring God
by Cruciform Press*

bit.ly/JOYPROJECT

"Biblically, colorfully, and with realistic precision, Tony Reinke presents God's work of saving grace as a jamboree of overwhelming sovereign joy. This is a book of deep truth that does good to the heart as well as the head."
J.I. Packer, Professor, Vancouver, British Columbia

"Our eyes of flesh seek joy in the wrong places, define it with a bankrupt vocabulary, and settle for it using mistaken formulas. All we know to do is try harder and hide our shame, we get stuck and sick, depressed and despondent. This dehumanizes, discourages, and defeats us. But there is hope! *The Joy Project* is applied reformed theology at its best."
Rosaria Champagne Butterfield, Author, The Gospel Comes with a House Key

"A unique and delightful summary of the unfolding drama of God's sovereign grace. Tony, as usual, is biblical, Christ-honoring, gospel-centric, imaginative, and articulate. Who could ask for more? You will enjoy this book!"
Randy Alcorn, Director, Eternal Perspective Ministries

"This is the most beautiful presentation of Calvinism I've ever read."
David Murray, Professor, Puritan Reformed Seminary

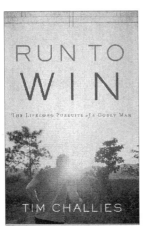

Run to Win
The Lifelong Pursuits of a Godly Man

by Tim Challies

Plan to run, train to run... run to win.

168 pages

bit.ly/RUN2WIN